The Weekend Quilt

Books by Leslie Linsley

The Weekend Quilt

Leslie Linsley

St. Martin's Press
New York

The Weekend Quilt

Preparation and design: Jon Aron Studio

Project director: Robby Smith
Illustrations: Peter Peluso, Jr.
Photography: Jon Aron
Quilt Designs: Jon Aron, Leslie Linsley, Robby Smith

Quilters:

Irish Chain	Ruth Linsley
Fence Rail	Elizabeth Mueller
Baby Gingham	Karen Chasteen
Four Square	Carol Sermerini
Mosaic Square	Connie Cicheti
Windmill	Carolyn Watts
Roman Square	Mary Beth Kaye
Around the World	Mary Chasteen
Country Roads	Phyllis Cohen
Squares and Blocks	Joan DeLue
Pinwheel	Frances Mueller
Shadow	Diane Lewis
Square Deal	Bonnie Burke
Crossroads	Enid Cherniak
Flying Geese	Corrinne Allesandrello
Harlequin	Ruth Linsley
Spinning Spools	Susan DeVault
Ohio Star	Mary Chasteen
Sampler	Thelma Goggins

Quilt photos taken on Nantucket Island

Library of Congress Cataloging-in-Publication Data

Linsley, Leslie.
  The weekend quilter.

  1. Quilting. I. Title.
TT835.L566 1986   746.9'7   86–1959
ISBN 0-312-86016-1

For information on how you can have *Better Homes & Gardens* magazine delivered to your door, write to:
Robert Austin, P.O. Box 4536, Des Moines, IA 50336.

Acknowledgments

I am especially grateful to the manufacturers who have been helpful in the preparation of this book. Their cooperation and interest in the project have been most generous. They are:

Fairfield Processing Corp., Danbury, Connecticut
Laura Ashley, New York, New York
Peter Pan Fabrics, New York, New York
VIP Fabrics, New York, New York

Contents

The Weekend Quilt

Introduction

"How much of my time is this going to take?" asked one of the ladies. My husband Jon and I were introducing a group of twelve women to the craft of quilting. None of them had ever made a quilt before and were understandably doubtful. "If you can sew a straight seam on a sewing machine you shouldn't have any trouble," we assured them. "These quilts have all been designed for quick-and-easy crafting."

Quiltmaking has become one of the most popular sewing crafts in this country today. Many of the quilts being stitched by home crafters imitate the familiar patterns designed by our earliest settlers. Those women had time for meticulous and detailed stitching. Making a quilt was a practical as well as a social activity. But today's quiltmakers find little extra time for crafting, although the desire to make a quilt is strongly felt. The simple elegance of patchwork quilts is appreciated for the warmth and interest it adds to any room.

Over the years a great many shortcuts have been employed for quiltmaking. *The Weekend Quilt* employs all these shortcuts for assembling and making quick quilts that don't look it.

All the women who made the quick quilts in this book were busy with demanding schedules. The premise was to teach them our quick techniques and to offer them each a design that would excite them so they would want to go on with the craft of quilting.

For months Jon and I designed patterns. My daughter Robby is now part of our team, having joined our studio this year following her college graduation. She worked with the patterns, designing and redesigning many of them to work within the premise. We visited many fabric showrooms to become familiar with the most up-to-date materials best suited for quilts. We arranged and rearranged colors and adjusted sizes so that the same patterns could be adapted to different bed sizes. Finally, we received much help in the form of information about products carried by various manufacturers to ease the quiltmaking processes. The results were then combined into the completion of nineteen quilts.

The women who made the quilts used our shortcuts and machine-stitched all the patchwork pieces for the quilt tops. They later hand-stitched the quilting because of an interest in extending the project to make more out of their quilts than originally intended. When they had completed one, many of the women wanted to make another quilt using one of the other patterns, and formed a group to meet regularly for quilting together. Three of the women went on vacation and used the time to quilt. And so our original weekend quilters quickly became hooked for longer periods.

I think that you'll find most of the patterns simple enough to piece the entire top in a weekend by using our helpful tips for cutting and assembling. Machine-piecing produces the accuracy needed for a precise quilt pattern, and there are many innovative ways to use the machine for shortcuts to piecing. Although piecing was done in its earliest form by hand, machine-pieced quilts date to as early as 1860.

Since the same patterns have been passed down through the generations, variations on each have evolved. Along the way, many quilters have solved basic problems by devising easier methods that benefit those who follow them. The choices of fabric colors are yours, so you can feel free to be creative with the patterns shown here by matching colors to your decorating scheme. In the event that you want to duplicate our quilts exactly, we have provided fabric information. The manufacturers of these fabrics distribute to fabric shops across the country or, in the case of Laura Ashley, offer a mail-order catalog. If we have used a particularly terrific tool or product for a technique, there will be a source for ordering it at the end of the book. And if you discover any shortcuts in the course of your quilting experience, please send them along to me so that I can, in turn, pass them along in subsequent books. Such is the nature of quiltmaking.

Quilting Terms

While there are many different kinds of quilts, some appliquéd, some made with patchwork, the following terms concern only those quilts that are shown in this book. The terms, materials, and techniques are fairly basic because these are all patchwork quilts made with triangles and squares.

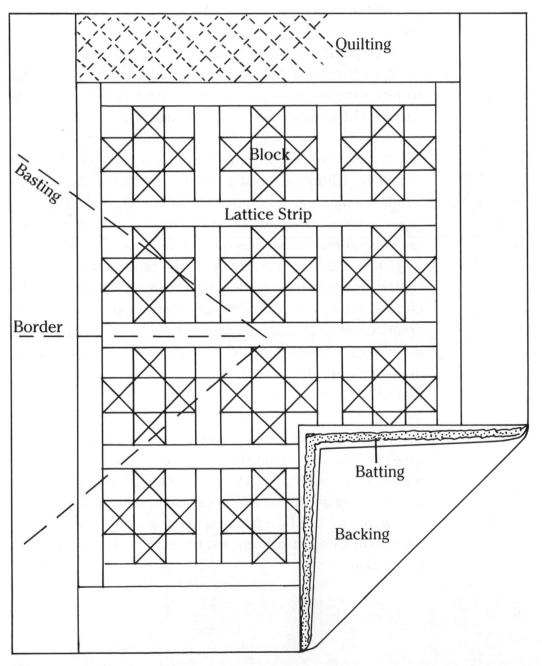

Backing: The bottom piece of fabric, which is of the same weight as the top. This piece can be a solid or printed fabric that matches the design on the top.

I often use old, softened sheets to back my quilts. My daughter sleeps under one and loves the feel of it. She eliminates a top sheet, which makes it easy to make the bed each morning. When using sheets it helps to have the exact size needed. Since most fabric is either 36 or 45 inches wide, it is almost always necessary to piece strips together for the backing.

The backing for all the quilts shown is unbleached muslin. This is an inexpensive material that is a neutral color. It often has sizing in it and requires a washing before attaching to the quilt. Many stitchers prefer muslin to sheeting as they say the needle goes through the fabric more easily.

Basting: Securing the top, batting, and backing together with long, loose stitches before quilting. These stitches are removed as each section is quilted.

Batting: The soft lining that makes the quilt puffy and gives it warmth. A quilt can be made with various thicknesses of batting. All our quilts were made with extra-loft®, 100 percent polyester POLY-FIL® from Fairfield Processing Corporation. This is a full, airy batting most often used for quilts. Fairfield also has a cotton batting and an ultra-loft® for extra thicknesses and double weight.

Binding: The way the raw edges of the quilt are finished. It can be done by cutting the backing slightly larger than the top. This piece is then brought forward, turned, and hemmed to the top, creating a finished border. Or, the top and back can be turned inward and stitched together. Another binding method is to sew a strip of contrasting fabric around the quilt by machine or hand, or to use a commercial binding tape in the color of your choice.

Block: Sometimes referred to as a square. Geometric or symmetrical pieces of fabric are sewn together to create a design. Finished blocks are sewn together, usually with a border (or sash) between each square.

Borders: Fabric strips that frame the pieced design. A border can be as narrow or wide as you like, depending on the size of the overall quilt and the size of the bed. There can be as many as three borders of the same or varying sizes and each can be made from different fabric patterns and colors. Borders are often used to extend the size of the quilt top so that it drops down on the sides, or can be folded over the bed pillows.

The borders used for our quilts are made up of continuous strips. None are pieced, as are the patchwork designs in the centers of the quilts.

Traditionally, quilting patterns are stitched in the borders. These can be made of a grid, circles, feathers, or interlocking swirls, to name a few.

Patchwork: Sewing together of fabric pieces to create an entire design. Sometimes the shapes form a geometric block. The blocks are then sewn together to make up the completed quilt. The quilts in this book are all made from squares and triangles that are pieced together to make the finished patchwork.

Piecing: Joining patchwork pieces together to form a design on the block.

Quilting: Stitching together two layers of fabric with a layer of batting between.

Quilting pattern: The lines or markings on the fabric that make up the design. Small hand or machine stitches quilt along these lines, which might be straight or curved or made up of elaborately curlicued patterns.

Sash or lattice strips: The narrow pieces of fabric used to frame the individual blocks and join them together. These are often of a contrasting color.

Setting: Joining the quilt blocks to form the finished top piece of the quilt.

Template: A pattern that is rigid and full size. It can be cut from cardboard or plastic and is used to trace the design elements. When cutting out the fabric, you will add a ¼-inch seam allowance. Very few quilts in this book will require a template, however, as we are working with triangles and squares.

Top: The top of a quilt is the front layer of fabric with the right side showing. The patchwork pieces create the quilt top.

Materials for Quiltmaking

Fabric: Almost every type of fabric has been used for making quilts. Experienced quilters, however, have narrowed the choices to those that have proven most effective. Cotton has and probably always will be the favored fabric for quilts, but a cotton blend or synthetic such as polyester is preferred by many. For best results, choose fabrics of the same fiber content and weight.

Pure cotton is the favorite because it wears well and is easy to work with. Because it shrinks, all cotton fabric should be washed before cutting. Unbleached muslin is often used for the back of a quilt. It is inexpensive and comes in various widths. It usually contains sizing and should be washed in very hot water and then machine-dried to pre-shrink. Press all fabric before beginning.

The colors and patterns of the fabric will greatly affect the quilt design. A combination of light and dark shades, for example, will produce a more flowing and subtle design.

Estimating amount of fabric: The directions for all quilts shown in this book include yardage for 45-inch-wide fabric. To determine your bed size, measure it fully made, that is, with bed pad, sheets, and blankets over the mattress. Measure the length, width, and depth, including the box spring. Decide if you want a slight overhang, an overhang with dust ruffle, or a drop to the floor, and whether the quilt will extend up and over the pillows.

To figure exact yardage, make a diagram on grid paper. One grid block represents 4 or 6 inches. Use this diagram as a guide when sewing together pieces for the final project. If the design shown for a quilt isn't adaptable to your bed size, you can add a border or reduce the size of an existing border.

Needles: These are often called "betweens." The sizes most commonly used are #7 and #8 Sharps.

Thread: If you can find it, cotton thread is best on cotton fabric. Polyester thread is more readily available, however, and I never seem to have a problem with it. Match the thread to the color of the fabric.

Pins: Fine, sharp pins are best for piecing fabric. I like the pins with a small ball head (because they are longer) for pinning fabric to batting.

Scissors: If you invest in good-quality scissors from the start, they will be the best quilting investment you'll ever make. This is especially true when cutting small pieces of fabric for patchwork. A good pair of scissors can cut a straight line of fabric without fraying or pulling it and will be more accurate.

I always keep a small pair of snipping scissors near my machine. When I do my piecing I try to snip away excess thread right then so I don't have to go back over the entire quilt searching for strays. This saves me time, but others prefer to do all snipping at the end.

Thimble: I've never gotten used to a thimble, but it's a handy tool if you are comfortable with it. One of the mail-order companies listed in the source list on page 158 has a product called Safety Stitcher for quilting tiny, neat stitches without sticking your fingers. It's a plastic finger guard that is adjustable in size.

Markers: Since these quilts are made of squares, you will be measuring and marking lines. I find a ballpoint pen the best for this. You will mark your lines on the wrong side of the fabric and if you cut carefully on the marked pin line you won't see the markings once the fabric is cut.

A soft pencil is good for tracing and transferring designs to the fabric. When marking your lines to follow for quilting this is fine. There are also water-soluble pens for this purpose. You can mark on the fabric, and when the quilt is finished any marks that show can be easily removed without scrubbing by simply using a plant mister.

Iron: It is impossible to do any sewing project without an iron. I've found it handy to pad a stool or chair with a piece of batting or newspaper and place it by my side at the sewing machine. As you piece the fabric you can iron the seams without getting up. Use a steam setting.

Frame or hoop: Most quilting can be done on a large hoop, but a full-size quilting frame is essential for many projects.

Some quilters find it most comfortable to quilt in their laps and can keep the tension of the stitches without a frame or hoop. Find the most efficient way for you. Hoops and frames are available in quilting stores and through mail-order sources (see page 158).

Cutting board: This is a handy item for the quick measuring and cutting methods you will use for the quilts in this book. It is available in fabric stores or from the mail-order sources listed on page 158.

Ruler and yardstick: A metal ruler is the most accurate way to measure and it provides the perfect straight edge against which to cut fabric or templates. It is also thin, so the measure lines are right on the fabric for accurate marking. A yardstick is also essential for marking and cutting strips that are the full width of the fabric. A yardstick is often used to mark a grid pattern on the fabric for quilting. The width of the yardstick is perfect for this and easy to handle. You simply draw the first line then flip the yardstick over and continue to mark lines without ever removing the yardstick from the fabric. You will have a perfect 1-inch grid.

Ripper: This isn't something we like to anticipate using, but it is inevitable that even the best stitcher will make an error. Some people find this a handy tool. I prefer sharp snipping scissors that are also used to trim loose threads at the beginning and end of piecing.

Quick-and-Easy Techniques

Marking board: To avoid marking and cutting each piece of fabric, it is helpful to make a marking and cutting board. This is a heavy piece of cardboard that will be divided into marked inch lines and used to measure and cut long strips of fabric. These strips will then be sewn together, marked, and cut so you end up with units of joined squares. This eliminates hours of cutting and sewing individual pieces. (See strip piecing page 20.)

Since fabric is 45 inches wide, it would seem best to use this measure for the size of your cardboard cutting board. Some stitchers, however, prefer to use a yardstick measure of 36 inches, since you will use the yardstick to mark off your inches. Probably the most practical is a board measuring 18 × 22 inches, which is a half yard of folded 45-inch-wide fabric. In this way, the cutting board isn't too cumbersome to fit on a table. The size of the cutting board isn't crucial; use the measure that is most comfortable.

Use your yardstick and mark inch lines across the top and bottom and along the sides of the cardboard. When cutting strips of fabric, this will help you to measure and lay the fabric out square. You can also use it to hold strips of fabric in place while matching and working with them.

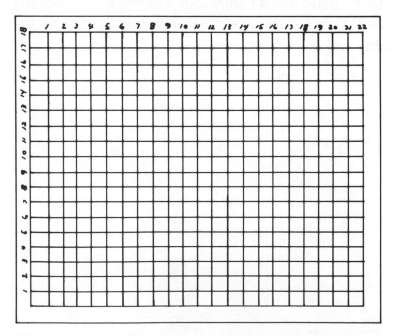

Sewing: All seams should be ¼ inch. If you place a piece of masking tape along the ¼-inch seam guide on your sewing machine, it will be an easy way to find it quickly and ensure accuracy.

Right triangles: There is a quick-and-easy way to join light and dark triangles to create squares of any size.

Once you've determined the size of your finished unit, you add 1 inch to it. For example, if you want to create 2-inch squares, you will add 1 inch and cut strips of light and dark fabric 3 inches wide by the length of your fabric, or the dimension given for each project.

Using your cutting board, place the two fabrics down with right sides facing up. Use your yardstick to draw a grid of 3-inch squares on the fabric.

Next, draw diagonal lines as per diagram. Stitch a ¼-inch seam on each side of the drawn diagonal lines as shown.

Cut on all solid lines to get the individual units of light and dark, or contrasting fabric triangles. Clip the corners, open, and press.

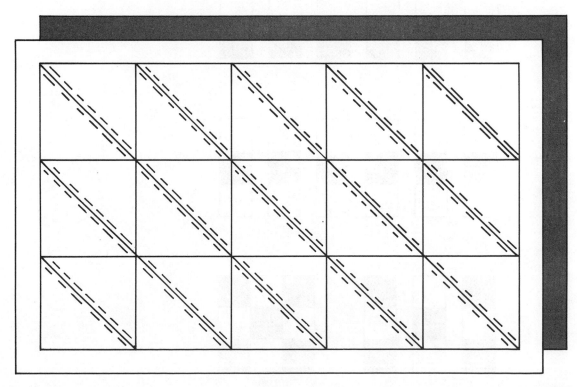

Strip piecing: This is the method by which you sew strips of different fabrics together and then cut them into units that are arranged to make up the entire quilt top. Rather than cutting and sewing individual squares together over and over again, two or more strips of fabric are sewn together and then cut into segments that are of the exact same dimensions. These units are then arranged and stitched together in different positions to form the quilt pattern.

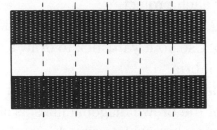

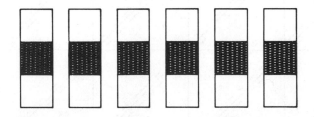

Template: Sometimes it is necessary to make a template for tracing design pieces. This is usually necessary when making an appliquéd quilt. Since we are concerned only with squares and triangles for patchwork here, the traditional template isn't needed. However, when doing strip piecing, where the project specifies 3½-inch-wide strips, for example, it is helpful to make a template rather than going to the trouble of making a cutting board.

A template can be made from cardboard or poster board. Simply measure and cut it to the width of the strip called for and the length of the cardboard. Use this to mark your fabric strips and you won't have to bother measuring over and over again. You'll always have an exact measure.

Quilting borders: When you want to fill large areas of the fabric with quilting, choose a simple design. This way, the quilting design won't compete with the patchwork design of the quilt.

There are several popular patterns used for background quilting. These include a feather, interlocking circles, shells, and grids. You can easily create circles or scallops to the desired size by using a compass. If a geometric print is used for the borders, an overall grid of squares or diamonds is preferred. Make a grid pattern with a yardstick or masking tape for accurate spacing.

Some of the mail-order sources that I've recommended supply templates for quilting patterns. This is an easy way to trace the quilting lines onto the fabric in order to machine- or hand-quilt.

Quilts to Make

Irish Chain

This is a popular early quilt pattern made up of squares put together. The two different fabric squares make up a nine-patch block. The Irish Chain is the perfect quilt pattern for strip piecing and is one of the easiest projects to make. The finished size is 63 × 81 inches.

Materials

(all fabric is 45 inches wide)
1½ yards dark fabric A
3½ yards light fabric B
4 yards fabric for backing
batting
thread to match fabric colors
needle for hand-quilting

Directions

Begin by cutting your fabric as follows:
A—15 strips 3½ × 42 inches
B—12 strips 3½ × 42 inches
B—31 squares 9½ × 9½ inches

Strip piecing

Unit #1 (refer to Fig. 1 as a guide).
1. With right sides facing and raw edges aligned, join 1 A strip to 1 B strip along one long edge, leaving a ¼-inch seam allowance.
2 Open seams and press.
3. Join another A strip to the B strip so you have one strip of light, dark, light fabric.

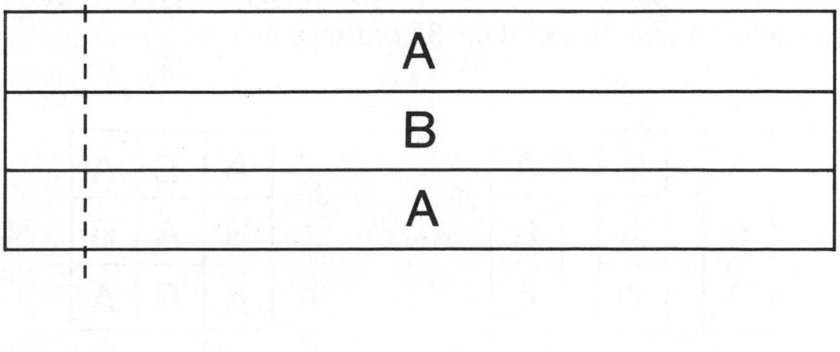

3½"

Fig. 1 Strip Piecing

| A |
| B |
| A |

4. Cut this strip into 3½-inch segments (see Fig. 2). There will be 12 segments.

5. Repeat steps 1 through 4 until you have 64 segments 3½ inches wide.

Unit #2 (refer to Fig. 3 as a guide).

6. Repeat steps 1 through 5, reversing the fabric order. In other words, stitch a light B strip to a dark A strip, followed by another B strip.

7. Cut into 3½-inch segments. There will be 12 segments. Continue to do this until you have 32 segments, each 3½ inches wide.

Fig. 2

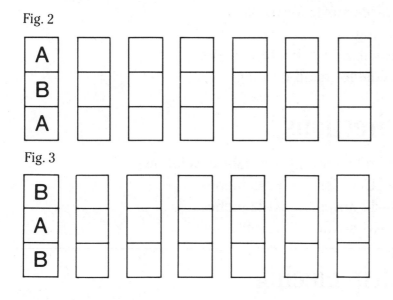

Fig. 3

To make a block

There are 32 pieced blocks in this quilt. Each block is 9 × 9 inches. Each pieced block is separated by a solid fabric block 9 × 9 inches, of which there are 31.

1. With right sides facing and raw edges aligned, stitch a unit #1 to a unit #2 along one long edge as shown in Fig. 4. Open seams and press.

2. Repeat with a unit #1 as shown in Fig. 4. You have now completed one block. Make 32 of these blocks.

Fig. 4

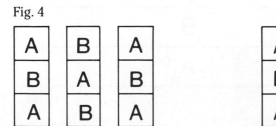

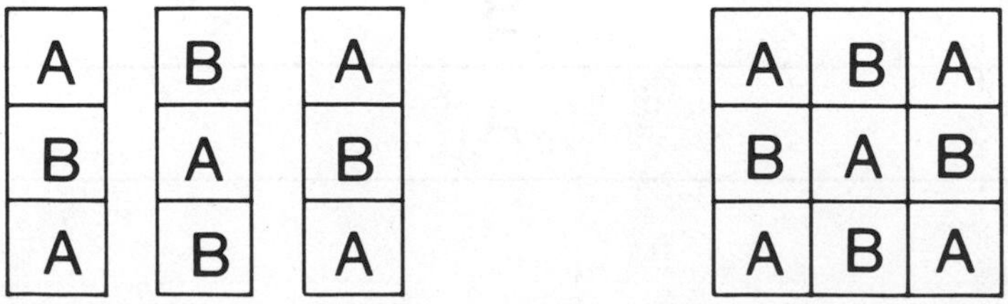

To make rows

1. With right sides facing and raw edges aligned, join a pieced block with a solid block as shown in Fig. 5.

2. Continue to join blocks in this way until you have a row of 4 pieced blocks separated by 3 solid blocks. Open and press seams.

3. Begin the next row with a solid block, followed by a pieced block, until you have joined 4 solid blocks divided by 3 pieced blocks.

4. Alternate rows in this way until you have made 9 rows of 7 blocks each.

Fig. 5

Joining rows

1. Refer to Fig. 6 to assemble, alternating rows. With right sides facing and raw edges aligned, stitch rows together horizontally.

2. Open all seams and press.

Fig. 6

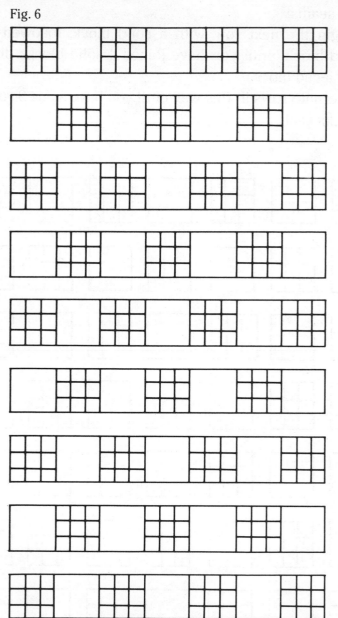

Preparing the backing

1. Cut the batting ¼-inch smaller than the quilt top all around.

2. Cut the 4 yards of backing fabric in half so you have two pieces of 2 yards each.

3. With right sides facing and raw edges aligned, stitch these pieces together along one long edge. You now have a backing piece that measures 72 × 90 inches.

4. Trim the backing to the quilt top size.

5. Baste the top, batting, and backing together with long stitches through all three layers. Begin at the center of the quilt and baste to each outer corner. If necessary to keep fabric from slipping, baste around outside edges as well.

Quilting

The quilting can be done on the machine if you want to finish the quilt quickly. Hand-stitching makes the quilt look better, however, and adds to the heirloom quality we admire in old quilts.

1. Begin at the center of the quilt to avoid bunching of the batting and work outward, taking small running stitches ¼ inch on either side of each seam line.

2. As you approach the outer edges of the quilt, stop stitching ½ inch before reaching the quilt edge so you have not stitched in the seam line. The raw edges will be turned under to finish the quilt.

3. To finish a line of quilting, pull the thread through to the backing side, make a small knot and pull back through the batting, popping the knot through the fabric. Clip the thread close to the quilt top. Or stitch over your last stitches several times to secure the end of the thread.

To finish

1. When all quilting is complete, clip basting stitches away.

2. Fold all raw edges of the top under ¼ inch and press. Fold the backing edges to the inside and press. Stitch together with a slipstitch, or blind stitch.

3. If you want a slight trim of the backing fabric all around the quilt top, fold the top edges under ½ inch and press.

4. Next bring the backing fabric forward and press ¼ inch all around. Fold again over the quilt top so there is a small (¼- to ½-inch) border all around. Stitch to the front of the quilt.

5. If bias tape is used to finish the edges, trim the backing to the same size as the top. Trim with matching or contrasting tape.

Fence Rail

This is a basic strip-piecing quilt. By putting three strips together—dark, light, medium—and piecing them according to the diagram, you will create a single Fence Rail pattern. The pattern is like steps going down the quilt. The effect is dark, light, medium. No matter what fabrics you use, it is recommended that you use this sequence to achieve the best results. This quilt is 54 × 84 inches, which is a twin size. It is easy to expand the quilt for a larger bed. Just continue the pattern or enlarge the borders.

Materials

(all fabric is 45 inches wide)
1 yard green calico A
1 yard white-and-rose colored calico B
1 yard solid rose fabric C
2½ yards brown calico D
3¼ yards fabric for backing
batting
thread to match fabric colors
needle for hand-quilting

Directions

Begin by cutting your fabric as follows:
A—14 strips 2½ × 45 inches
B—14 strips 2½ × 45 inches
C—14 strips 2½ × 45 inches
D—2 pieces 6½ × 42½ inches for top and bottom border
D—2 pieces 6½ × 84½ inches for side border

Strip piecing

Refer to Fig. 1 as a guide.
1. With right sides facing and raw edges aligned, join 1 A strip to 1 B strip along one long edge, leaving a ¼-inch seam allowance.
2. Open seams and press.
3. Join a C strip to the B strip to make an ABC strip.
4. Repeat steps 1 through 3 with all A, B, C fabric strips.
5. Cut the strips into 6½-inch segments to make squares (see Fig. 1). You will have 84 squares.

A
B
C

To make rows

1. Refer to Fig. 2 in order to arrange the individual squares in a horizontal row. With right sides facing and raw edges aligned, stitch the first 2 squares together.
2. Open seams and press.
3. Continue to join squares in this way as per Fig. 2.
4. Next sew 7 squares together arranged as in Fig. 3.
5. Make a total of 6 rows of each arrangement of squares.

Fig. 2

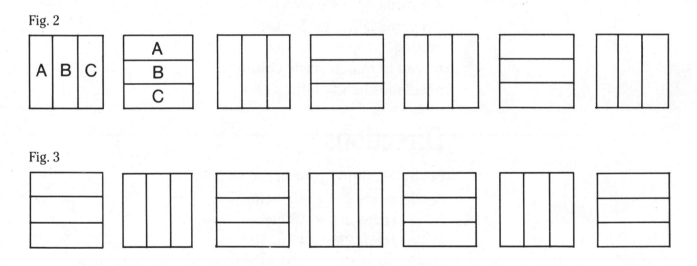

Fig. 3

Joining rows

1. With right sides facing and edges aligned, join row #1 with row #2 as per Fig. 4.
2. Open seams and press.
3. Continue to join rows in this alternating way until all 12 rows are joined, ending with a row #2.
4. Open all seams and press.

Fig. 4

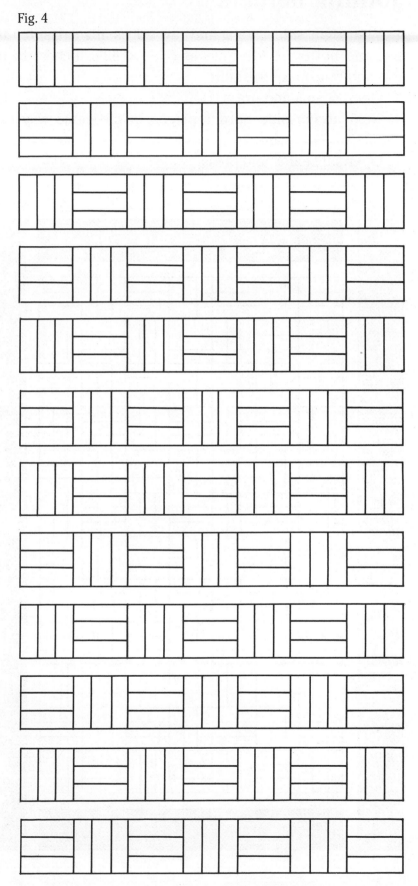

Joining borders

1. With right sides facing and raw edges aligned, stitch the top and bottom border pieces (6½ × 42½ inches) to the top and bottom of the quilt.
2. Open seams and press.
3. Next attach side border pieces in the same way (see Fig. 5).
4. Open all seams and press.

Fig. 5

Preparing the backing

1. Cut the batting ½ inch smaller than the quilt top all around.
2. Cut the backing fabric in half so you have two equal pieces, each 1⅝ yards.
3. With right sides facing and raw edges aligned, stitch these pieces together to make one piece of fabric the same size as the quilt top. Trim extra fabric all around backing, if necessary.
4. Baste the top, batting, and backing together with long stitches through all three layers. Begin at the center of the quilt and baste to each outer corner. Baste around outside edges, if necessary.

Quilting

1. Begin at the center of the quilt and work outward taking small running stitches ¼ inch on both sides of each seam line. If you machine-quilt, follow the seam line and stitch in the channel.
2. Stop the stitches ½ inch before reaching edges.
3. You can create a quilting pattern in the border, if desired. To do this refer to page 21 for transferring a pattern or creating a grid to follow when stitching.

To finish

1. When all quilting is complete, clip basting stitches away.
2. Fold all raw edges of the top under ¼ inch and press. Fold the backing edges to the inside and press. Stitch together with a slipstitch, or machine-stitch all around.
3. Press around outer edge of entire quilt.
Note: If you'd like a nicely finished turned edge on the quilt top, attach the backing before quilting in the following way:
1. With right sides facing, stitch backing to quilt top and batting by sewing around the edges, leaving 12 inches open for turning.
2. Turn fabric right side out and press all around.
3. Baste all three layers of fabric together and quilt along seam lines as before.

Gingham Baby Coverlet

This baby coverlet, made from different gingham fabric colors, is easy and expandable. Since it is made up of squares, you can make it to fit a carriage, crib, or youth bed. You can use any fabrics, solid or printed, in delicate colors. By using only nine squares you can make a pillow cover to match. This is a wonderful weekend project. The finished size is 39 × 39 inches and will fit a crib.

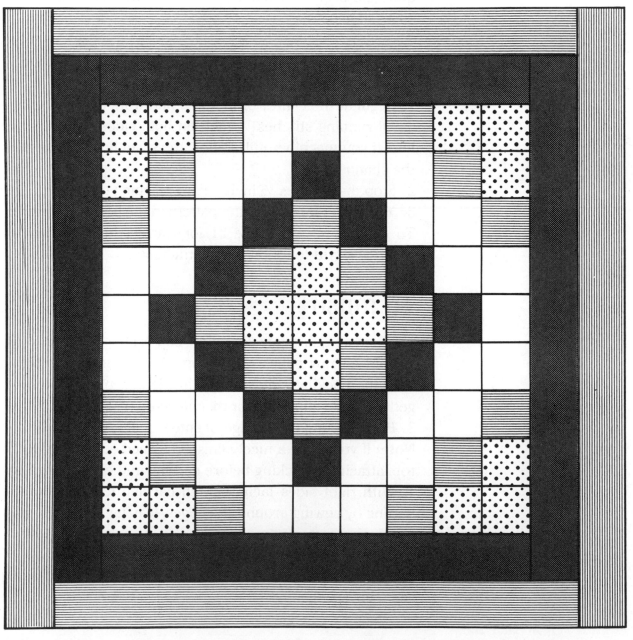

Materials

(all fabric is 45 inches wide)
½ yard yellow gingham A   —green
1 yard pink gingham B   —red
1 yard blue gingham C — blue
½ yard white fabric D — white print
1½ yards backing fabric
batting
thread to match fabric colors
needle for hand-quilting

Directions

Cut all border pieces as follows:
B—2 pieces 3½ × 33½ inches for top and bottom ⟩ yellow
B—2 pieces 3½ × 39½ inches for the sides
C—2 pieces 3½ × 27½ inches for top and bottom
C—2 pieces 3½ × 33½ inches for the sides
Cut the following number of squares 3½ × 3½ inches:
A—17 squares
B—20 squares
C—12 squares
D—32 squares

To make a row

1. With right sides facing and raw edges aligned, stitch 2 A squares together along one side.
2. Open seams and press.
3. Refer to Fig. 1 and join a B square, followed by 3 D squares, then a B square, followed by 2 A squares, for a total of 9 squares in the row.
4. Open all seams and press.

Fig. 1

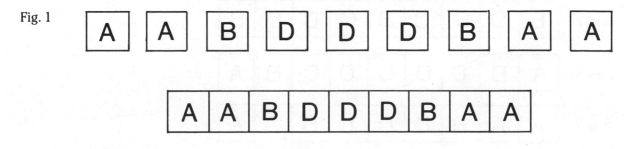

37

5. Continue with 8 more rows. The following is the pattern sequence:

Row 2: A-B-D-D-C-D-D-B-A
Row 3: B-D-D-C-B-C-D-D-B
Row 4: D-D-C-B-A-B-C-D-D
Row 5: D-C-B-A-A-A-B-C-D
Row 6: D-D-C-B-A-B-C-D-D
Row 7: B-D-D-C-B-C-D-D-B
Row 8: A-B-D-D-C-D-D-B-A
Row 9: A-A-B-D-D-D-B-A-A

Joining rows

1. With right sides facing and raw edges aligned, join row #1 with row #2 along the bottom long edge.
2. Open seams and press.
3. Refer to Fig. 2 and continue to join the rows in the same way.
4. Open all seams and press.

Fig. 2

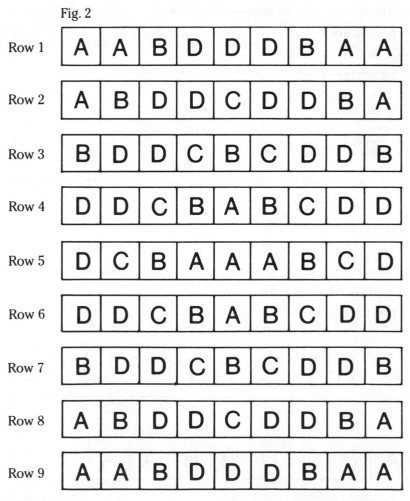

Row 1	A	A	B	D	D	D	B	A	A
Row 2	A	B	D	D	C	D	D	B	A
Row 3	B	D	D	C	B	C	D	D	B
Row 4	D	D	C	B	A	B	C	D	D
Row 5	D	C	B	A	A	A	B	C	D
Row 6	D	D	C	B	A	B	C	D	D
Row 7	B	D	D	C	B	C	D	D	B
Row 8	A	B	D	D	C	D	D	B	A
Row 9	A	A	B	D	D	D	B	A	A

Joining borders

1. With right sides facing and raw edges aligned, stitch the top and bottom C border strips to the top and bottom of the quilt top (see Fig. 3).
2. Open seams and press.
3. Join side C border strips in the same way.

Fig. 3

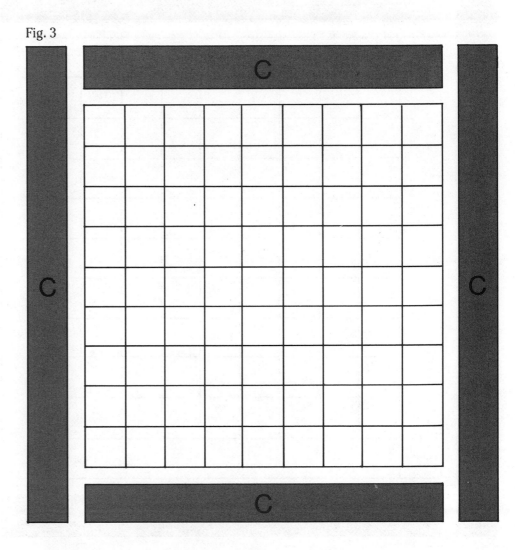

4. Next join the top and bottom B border strips to the top and bottom of the quilt top (see Fig. 4).

5. Open seams and press.

6. Join side B border strips in the same way.

7. Open all seams and press.

Fig. 4

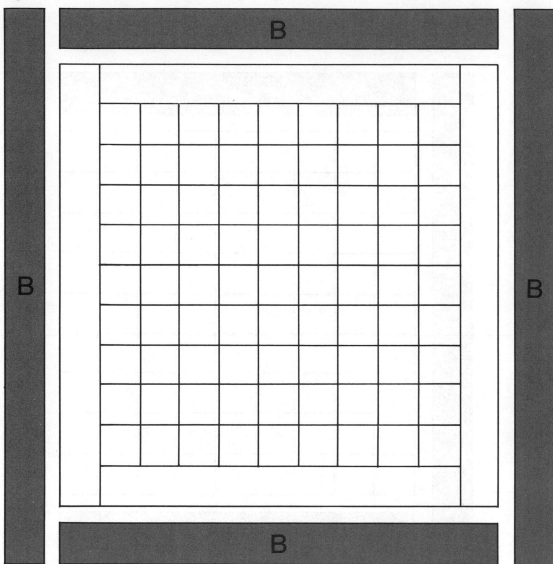

Preparing the backing

1. Cut the batting ½ inch smaller than the quilt top all around.
2. Baste the quilt top and the batting together with long loose stitches.
3. Pin the backing to the front of the quilt top and stitch around 3 sides and 4 corners, leaving 12 inches open on one edge for turning.
4. Clip corners and trim edges close to the seam line.
5. Turn the quilt right side out so that the batting is between the quilt top and backing fabric.
6. Press all around the edges.

Quilting

1. To hand-quilt, begin at the center of the top and work outward, taking small running stitches ¼ inch on either side of each seam line.
2. To quilt by machine, baste the three layers of fabric together to keep the batting and backing from bunching. Stitch along all seam lines of each gingham square and along the border seams.

To finish

1. When all quilting is complete, clip the basting stitches away.
2. Press the quilt and turn the opening edge of the top and backing to the inside ¼ inch. Press.
3. Slipstitch opening closed.

Four Square

This quilt is made up of 4-inch squares and is the ideal pattern for a large quilt. You can use the quick cut-and-strip piecing method, but the squares are large and therefore easy to sew separately. The finished size is 80 × 96 inches and is intended to fit a double or queen-size bed. If you use this pattern for a twin-size bed it will look just as good and is a cinch to make.

Materials

(all fabric is 45 inches wide)
1½ yards dark brown calico A
1½ yards light brown calico B
1½ yards rust-colored calico C
1½ yards white calico D
5½ yards backing material
batting
thread to match fabric colors
needle for hand-quilting

Directions

Begin by cutting the following:
A—12 strips 4½ × 45 inches
A—5 squares 4½ × 4½ inches
B—12 strips 4½ × 45 inches
B—5 squares 4½ × 4½ inches
C—12 strips 4½ × 45 inches
C—5 squares 4½ × 4½ inches
D—12 strips 4½ × 45 inches
D—5 squares 4½ × 4½ inches

Strip piecing

1. With right sides facing and raw edges aligned, join 1 A strip to 1 B strip, with a ¼-inch seam allowance.
2. Open seams and press.
3. Join 1 C strip to 1 D strip in the same way.
4. Refer to Fig. 1 and cut the joined strips into 4½-inch segments. You will need 115 A-B segments and 115 C-D segments.

Fig. 1 Strip Piecing

4½"

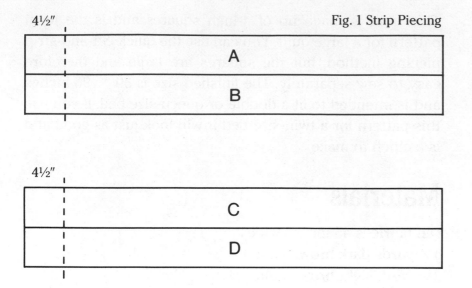

4½"

To make rows

1. Refer to Fig. 2. To make the first vertical row, stitch an A-B segment to a C-D segment. Continue to join alternating segments until you have joined 12.

2. Open seams and press. Make 5 of these rows.

3. For vertical row #2, join a single D square with an A-B segment as shown in Fig. 2. Alternate A-B and C-D segments, finishing with a C square on the bottom of the row.

4. Open seams and press. Make 5 of these rows.

5. Row #3 is made of alternating C-D and A-B segments. Make 5 of these. Open seams and press.

6. Begin row #4 by joining a B square at the top of a C-D segment as shown in Fig. 2. Next join an A-B segment, alternating segments and finishing with an A square at the bottom.

7. Open all seams and press. Make 5 of these rows.

Fig. 2

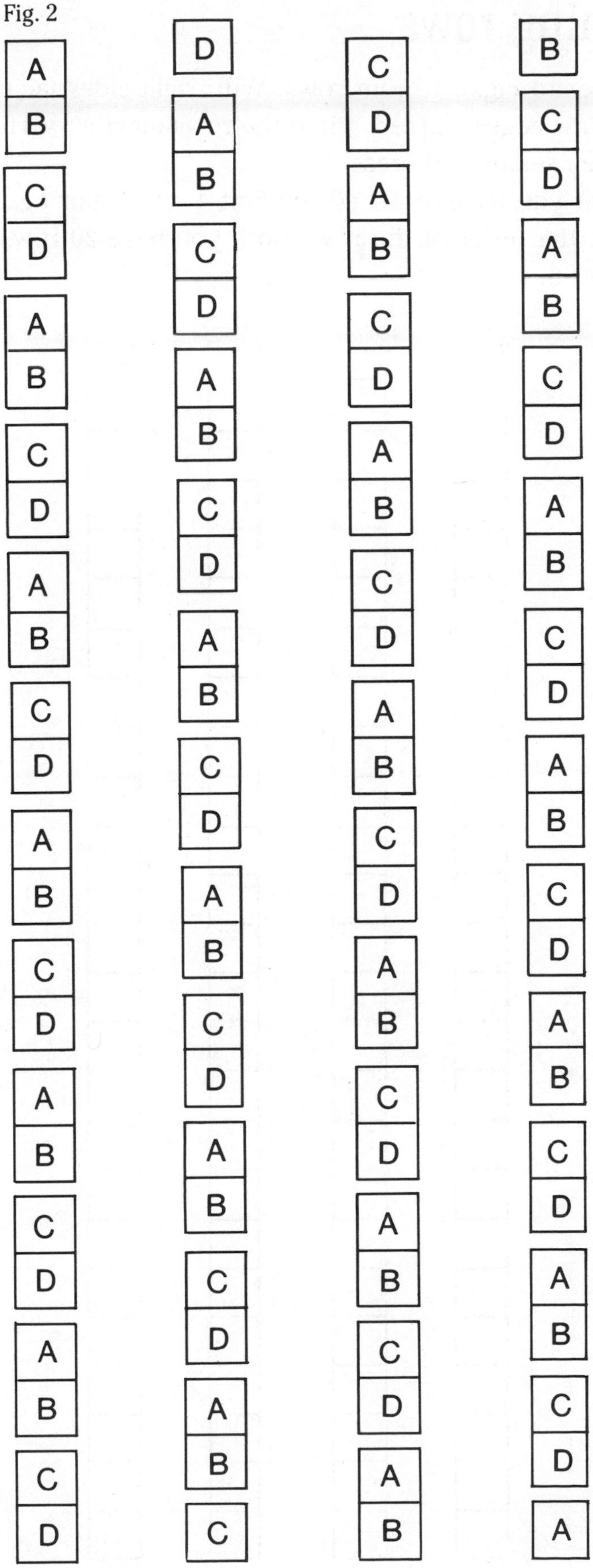
A B C D A B C D A B C D A B C D A B C D A B C D
D A B C D A B C D A B C D A B C D A B C D A B C
C D A B C D A B C D A B C D A B C D A B C D A B
B C D A B C D A B C D A B C D A B C D A B C D A

Joining rows

1. Refer to Fig. 3 to join rows. With right sides facing and long, raw edges aligned, stitch the rows together vertically.
2. Open seams and press.
3. After you have attached the first 4 rows, start again and repeat the order of the rows until you have 20 rows of 24 squares in each.

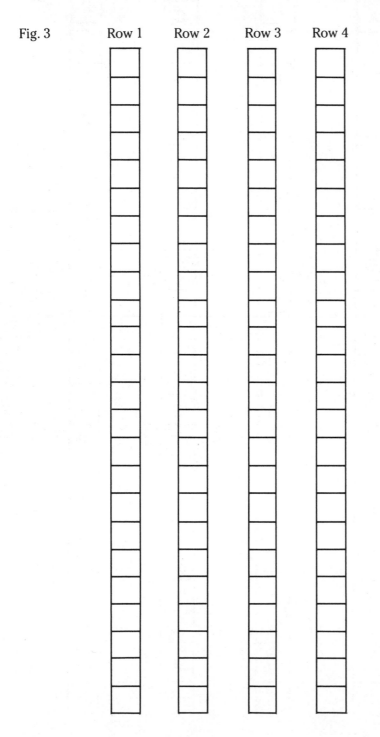

Fig. 3   Row 1   Row 2   Row 3   Row 4

Preparing the backing

1. Cut the batting ¼ inch smaller than the quilt top all around.
2. Cut the backing in half so you have two pieces 2¾ yards each.
3. With right sides facing and raw edges aligned, stitch these pieces together along one long edge. You now have a backing piece to fit your quilt.
4. Trim to quilt top size.
5. Baste the top, batting, and backing together with long stitches through all three layers. Begin at the center and baste to each outer corner of the quilt. Pin or baste around outer edges.

Quilting

If you are making this quilt for a king-size bed you may want to quilt by machine-stitching in all seam lines. If you want to quilt by hand you might find this a relaxing lap project to do in your spare moments.

1. Begin at the center of the quilt and work outward, taking small running stitches ¼ inch on each side of all seam lines.
2. Keep stitches from entering the seam line at the outer edges of the quilt, as the raw edges will be turned to the inside to finish.

To finish

1. When all quilting is complete, clip basting stitches away.
2. Fold all raw edges of the top under ¼ inch and press. Fold the backing edges to the inside and press. Stitch together with a slipstitch, or machine-stitch close to the edge of the quilt.
3. If you've used a decorative backing fabric, you might want to have a slight trim showing all around the top edges of the quilt. Fold the top edges under ½ inch and press. Bring the backing fabric forward and press ¼ inch under all around. Fold again over the quilt top and stitch to the front.
4. Press all quilt edges.

Mosaic Square

This quilt is made up of squares put together to form a larger square. A blue color scheme was used here, but you can get the same effect with any color. Simply follow the placement of light and dark shades. The symmetrical design can be continued to any size in order to make it fit your bed. This 60-inch square makes a nice wallhanging.

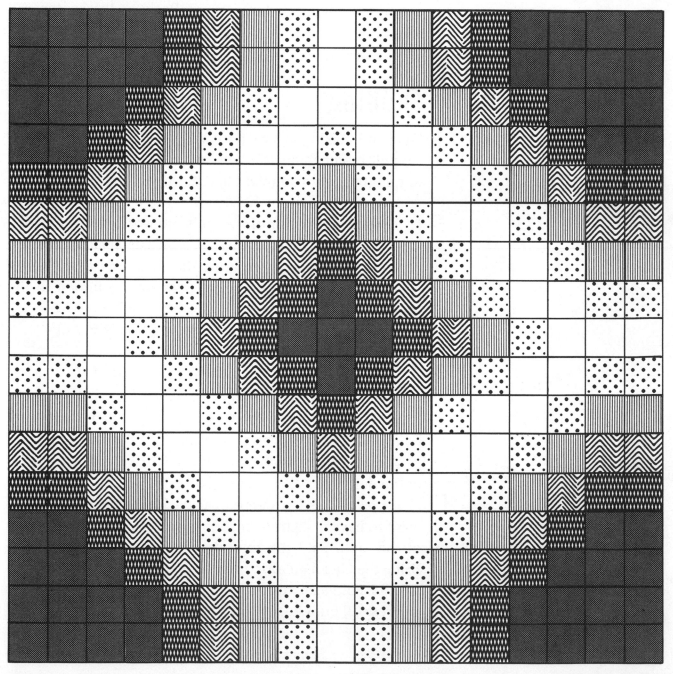

Materials

(all fabric is 45 inches wide)
1 yard navy blue fabric A
1 yard dark blue floral print B
1 yard royal blue floral print C
1 yard light blue floral print D
1 yard turquoise floral print E
1 yard white with blue print F
batting
3½ yards backing fabric
thread to match fabric colors
needle for hand-quilting

Directions

All squares are 4 × 4 inches when finished. Be sure to cut each one 4½ × 4½ inches to allow for a ¼-inch seam on all sides. You will need the following:
A—29 squares
B—24 squares
C—32 squares
D—40 squares
E—48 squares
F—52 squares

To make rows

Refer to Fig. 1 when arranging the squares in a row.
1. With right sides facing and raw edges aligned, stitch an A square to another A square. Open seams and press.
2. Continue to add squares in this way to make a horizontal row of 15 according to Fig. 1.
3. Open seams and press. Continue to make 15 rows of 15 squares. Refer to Fig. 2 for pattern sequence.

Note: When cutting out squares consider using a cutting board and cardboard template. Cut a strip of posterboard 4½ inches wide by the length of your fabric. Place the fabric on the cutting board and use the cardboard to make a grid of 4½-inch squares. Use a rotary cutting wheel (see source list) to zip through the cutting of all fabric pieces.

Fig. 1

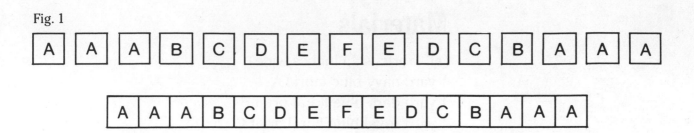

| A | A | A | B | C | D | E | F | E | D | C | B | A | A | A |

| A | A | A | B | C | D | E | F | E | D | C | B | A | A | A |

Joining rows

1. With right sides facing and raw edges aligned, stitch row #1 to row #2 along one long edge.

2. Open seams and press.

3. Repeat by joining row #3 to row #2 in the same way. Continue to join all rows in this way as per Fig. 2.

4. Open all seams and press.

Fig. 2

A	A	A	B	C	D	E	F	E	D	C	B	A	A	A	Row 1
A	A	B	C	D	E	F	F	F	E	D	C	B	A	A	Row 2
A	B	C	D	E	F	F	E	F	F	E	D	C	B	A	Row 3
B	C	D	E	F	F	E	D	E	F	F	E	D	C	B	Row 4
C	D	E	F	F	E	D	C	D	E	F	F	E	D	C	Row 5
D	E	F	F	E	D	C	B	C	D	E	F	F	E	D	Row 6
E	F	F	E	D	C	B	A	B	C	D	E	F	F	E	Row 7
F	F	E	D	C	B	A	A	A	B	C	D	E	F	F	Row 8
E	F	F	E	D	C	B	A	B	C	D	E	F	F	E	Row 9
D	E	F	F	E	D	C	B	C	D	E	F	F	E	D	Row 10
C	D	E	F	F	E	D	C	D	E	F	F	E	D	C	Row 11
B	C	D	E	F	F	E	D	E	F	F	E	D	C	B	Row 12
A	B	C	D	E	F	F	E	F	F	E	D	C	B	A	Row 13
A	A	B	C	D	E	F	F	F	E	D	C	B	A	A	Row 14
A	A	A	B	C	D	E	F	E	D	C	B	A	A	A	Row 15

Preparing the backing

1. Cut the batting ¼ inch smaller than the quilt top all around.
2. Cut the backing fabric in half so you have two pieces of 1¾ yards each.
3. With right sides facing and raw edges aligned, stitch these pieces together along one long edge to create the backing for the quilt top.
4. Baste the top, batting, and backing together with long stitches through all three layers. Begin at the center of the quilt and baste to each outer corner.
5. Pin or baste around the outside edges.

Quilting

1. To hand-quilt, begin at the center of the top and work outward taking small running stitches ¼ inch on both sides of each seam line. End the stitches ½ inch before the seam line at the edges of the quilt.
2. To quilt by machine, stitch along the seam line of each square, taking care that the batting does not bunch up.

To finish

1. When all quilting is complete, clip the basting stitches away.
2. Fold the raw edges of the top under ¼ inch and press. Turn backing fabric to the inside ¼ inch and press. Stitch together with a slipstitch, or machine-stitch all around.

Windmill

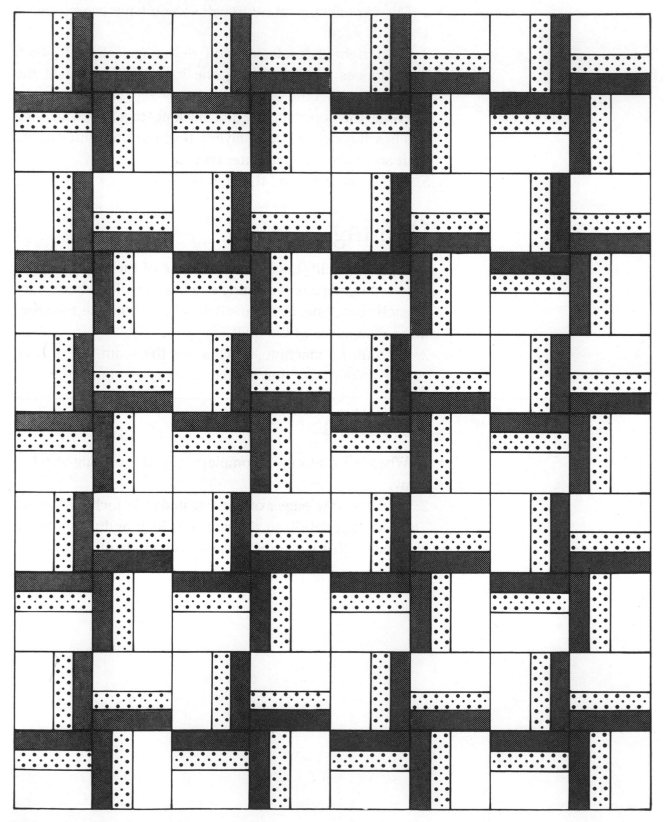

The windmill pattern is one of the easiest to cut, piece, and stitch together. You will be using the strip method of quilting. Each block is made up of three rectangles. Two of the rectangular strips are equal to the size of the third. The strips that are joined to make the windmill design are made from dark fabric, with the light fabric at each outside corner of the block.

The finished size is 80 × 100 inches and will fit a double or queen-size bed. To make it a king-size, simply add a border around the outside to add the inches needed. Or add another row of blocks. To make this pattern fit a twin, eliminate a vertical row of blocks.

Materials

(all fabric is 45 inches wide)
2 yards dark blue fabric A
2 yards red fabric B
3½ yards white fabric C
6 yards fabric for backing
batting
thread to match fabric colors
needle for hand-quilting

Directions

Begin by cutting your fabric as follows:
A—20 strips 3 × 42 inches
B—20 strips 3 × 42 inches
C—20 strips 5½ × 42 inches

Strip piecing

1. With right sides facing and raw edges aligned, join 1 A strip to 1 B strip along one long edge leaving a ¼-inch seam allowance.
2. Open seams and press.

3. Repeat with 1 C strip attached to the B strip in the same way so you have two dark strips and a light strip.

4. Cut the strip unit into 10½-inch segments (see Fig. 1). There will be 4 segments.

5. Continue to do this until you have 80 segments, which we will now refer to as squares.

10½″   Fig. 1 Strip Piecing

| A |
| B |
| C |

To make a block

Each block is made up of 4 squares. Refer to Fig. 2 in order to arrange the squares into blocks.

1. With right sides facing and raw edges aligned, sew 4 squares together as per Fig. 2.

2. Open seams and press.

3. Continue to sew 4 squares together to make 20 blocks.

Fig. 2

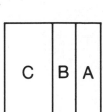

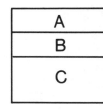

To make a row

1. Refer to Fig. 3 to join blocks. With right sides facing and raw edges aligned, stitch the blocks together to make a horizontal row of 4 blocks.
2. Continue to join blocks in this way until you have 5 rows of 4 blocks each.
3. Open all seams and press.

Fig. 3

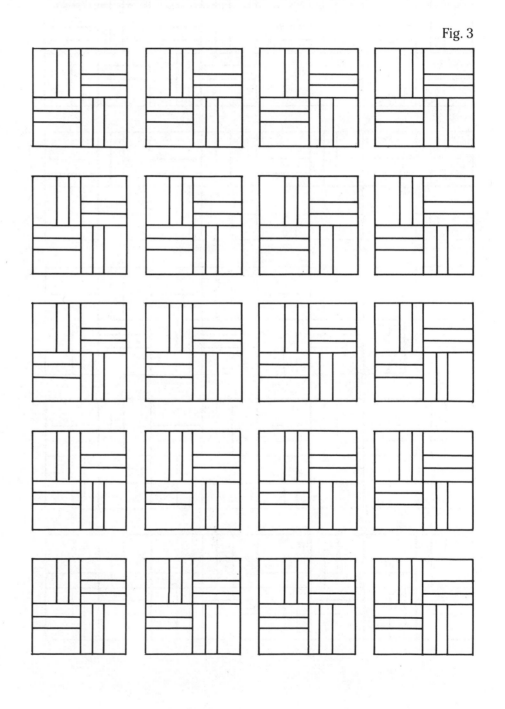

Joining rows

1. With right sides facing and long raw edges aligned, stitch row #1 to row #2 as shown in Fig. 4. Open seams and press.
2. Continue to join rows in this way to finish the top of the quilt.

Fig. 4

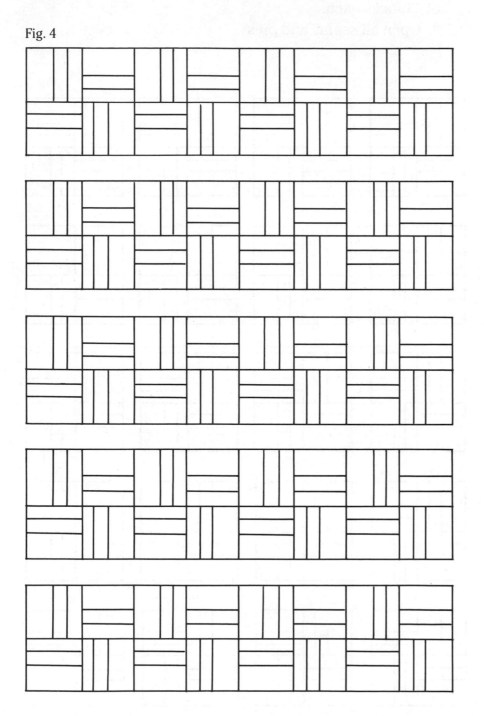

Preparing the backing

Note: If you would like to add a border to this quilt you will have to decide this before cutting the backing material so that the backing size can accommodate the added inches created by the borders.

1. Cut the batting ¼ inch smaller than the quilt top all around.

2. Cut the backing material in half so you have two 3-yard pieces.

3. With right sides facing and long edges aligned, stitch the backing pieces together so you have a piece of fabric 90 × 108 inches.

4. Trim the backing fabric to the size of the quilt top.

5. With the quilt top face up on top of the batting and backing fabric, baste all three layers together with long stitches. Begin at the center of the quilt and baste to each outer corner. If necessary to keep fabric from slipping, baste around outside edges as well.

Quilting

1. Begin at the center of the quilt and work outward, taking small running stitches ¼ inch on both sides of each seam line. If you are doing this on the machine, set the stitch setting for a long stitch, or simply stitch along the seam channel rather than on either side of the seam line.

2. As you approach the outer edges of the quilt, stop the stitches ½ inch before reaching quilt edge.

3. To finish a line of hand-quilting, pull the thread through to the backing side, make a small knot, and pull back through the batting, popping the knot through the fabric. Clip the thread close to the quilt top.

To finish

1. When all quilting is complete, clip away the basting stitches.

2. Fold the raw edges of the top under ¼ inch and press. Fold the backing edges to the inside and press. Stitch together with a slipstitch or blind stitch.

Roman Square

Made with red, white, and blue fabric, this pattern is similar to the Fence Rail quilt. It is one of the easiest patterns in the book and is made with the strip-piecing method. The finished quilt measures 66 × 80 inches and will fit a double or queen-size bed. It is very simple to make it larger or smaller by adding or eliminating blocks, or by adjusting the surrounding border. For an even simpler version, eliminate the lattice strips between each square and you will have the perfect weekend quilt.

Materials

(all fabric is 45 inches wide)
2½ yards red floral print A
1 yard blue-and-white pinstripe fabric B
1 yard solid blue fabric C
2½ yards white fabric D
2½ yards blue-and-white floral print E
4 yards backing fabric
batting
thread to match fabric colors
needle for hand-quilting

Directions

Begin by cutting all fabric as follows:
A—2 pieces 1½ × 80½ inches for side borders
A—2 pieces 1½ × 64½ inches for top and bottom borders
A—14 strips 2½ × 39 inches
B—14 strips 2½ × 39 inches
C—14 strips 2½ × 39 inches
D—2 pieces 2½ × 72½ inches for side borders
D—6 pieces 2½ × 54½ inches for top, middle, and bottom borders and lattice strips
D—15 pieces 2½ × 12½ inches
E—2 pieces 3½ × 78½ inches for side borders
E—2 pieces 3½ × 58½ inches for top and bottom borders

1. With right sides facing and raw edges aligned, sew an A strip to a B strip along one long edge.

2. Open seams and press.

3. Next, attach a C strip to the B strip in the same way. Open seams and press.

4. Refer to Fig. 1 and cut the strips into 6½-inch segments to make squares.

5. Continue to do this with all the strips in order to make 80 squares.

6½″   Fig. 1 Strip Piecing

| A |
| B |
| C |

To make a block

1. Each block is made up of 4 squares. Refer to Fig. 2 for the arrangement of squares, and with right sides facing and raw edges aligned, stitch 2 squares together along one edge.

2. Open seams and press.

3. With right sides facing and raw edges aligned, stitch the next 2 squares of the block together.

4. Open seams and press.

5. Join the 4 squares in the same way. Open all seams and press.

6. Continue to make 20 blocks in this way.

Fig. 2

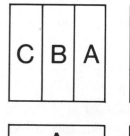
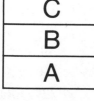
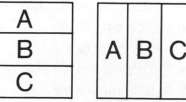

To make a row

1. With right sides facing and raw edges aligned, stitch a block to a 2½ × 12½-inch D lattice strip along one long edge as shown in Fig. 3.
2. Open seams and press.
3. Next, join the second block in the same way and continue to add 2 more blocks separated by lattice strips. There will be 4 blocks and 3 lattice strips in the horizontal row.
4. Open all seams and press.
5. Continue to make 5 rows of 4 blocks each in this way.

Fig. 3

Joining rows

1. With right sides facing and raw edges aligned, join row #1 and a 2½ × 54½-inch D border strip across the top long edge as shown in Fig. 4.

2. Open seams and press.

3. Continue to join rows with a D lattice strip between. Open seams and press.

4. Attach the last D border to the bottom edge of the last row. Open seams and press.

5. With right sides facing and edges aligned, stitch side D border pieces (2½ × 72½ inches) to each side edge of the quilt top.

6. Open seams and press.

Fig. 4

Joining borders

1. With right sides facing and raw edges aligned, stitch the top and bottom 3½ × 58½-inch E border pieces to the top and bottom of the quilt along the outside raw edge (see Fig. 5).

2. Open seams and press.

3. Next, attach side border pieces E in the same way. Open seams and press.

Fig. 5

4. With right sides facing and raw edges aligned, stitch the top and bottom 1½ × 64½-inch A borders to the top and bottom of the quilt along the outside raw edge as shown in Fig. 6.

5. Open seams and press.

6. Next, attach the side border pieces A in the same way. Open seams and press.

A

Fig. 6

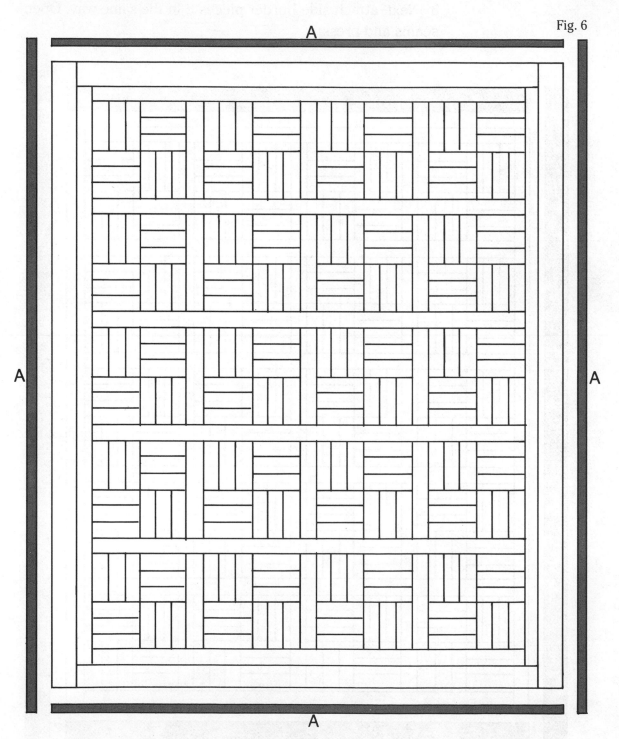

A

A

A

Irish Chain (page 24)

Fence Rail (page 30)

Roman Square (page 58)

Four Square (page 42)

Around the World (page 66)

Baby Gingham Coverlet (page 36)

Windmill (page 52)

Mosaic Square (page 48)

Flying Geese (page 118)

Shadow (page 94)

Pinwheel (page 88)

Square Deal (page 102)

Squares and Blocks (page 80)

Country Roads (page 72)

Crossroads (page 110)

Ohio Star (page 140)

Harlequin (page 124)

Spinning Spools (page 130)

Sampler (page 148)

Preparing the backing

1. Cut the batting ½ inch smaller than the quilt top all around.

2. Cut the backing fabric in half so you have two equal pieces of 2 yards each.

3. With right sides facing and raw edges aligned, stitch these pieces together to make one piece of fabric the same size as the quilt top. Trim extra fabric all around backing if necessary.

4. Baste the top, batting, and backing together with long stitches through all three layers. Begin at the center of the quilt and baste to each outer corner. Baste around outside edges, if necessary.

Quilting

1. Begin at the center of the quilt and work outward taking small running stitches a ¼ inch on both sides of each seam line of each striped piece of fabric. Quilt along the border seam lines as well.

2. To quilt by machine, stitch along the seam line of each strip and joining seams of each block.

3. To quilt the borders see page 21.

To finish

1. When all quilting is complete, clip basting stitches away.

2. Fold all raw edges of the top under ¼ inch and press. Fold the backing edges to the inside and press.

3. Stitch together with a slipstitch, or machine-stitch all around.

Around the World

This dynamic quilt is made of rich, colorful earth tones to give it a textured appearance. Laura Ashley fabrics are used for a variety of interest. This is an example of how you can take a simple technique of sewing squares together and concentrate on designing with fabric patterns and colors to create a sophisticated-looking quilt. Even though the squares are set on the diagonal, this is no harder than putting squares together. The finished size is 75 × 75 inches and will fit a double or queen-size bed.

Materials

(all fabric is 45 inches wide)
1 yard fabric A
½ yard fabric B
1 yard fabric C
½ yard fabric D
½ yard fabric E
½ yard fabric F
1 yard fabric G
1 yard fabric H
4 yards backing material
batting
thread to match fabric colors
needle for hand-quilting

Directions

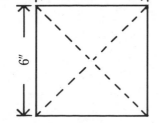

All squares are 5½ × 5½ inches, allowing for a ¼-inch seam all around. The triangles are cut from 6-inch squares. Begin by cutting your fabric as follows:

A—5 squares 5½ × 5½ inches
A—19 squares 6 × 6 inches

> Cut 18 of the 6-inch squares in half on the diagonal to create 36 triangles of A fabric. Cut the remaining 6-inch square to make 4 triangles (see Fig. 1).

Fig. 1

6"

6"

All squares that follow should be cut 5½ × 5½ inches in the following numbers.

B—8 squares
C—48 squares
D—16 squares
E—20 squares
F—24 squares
G—28 squares
H—32 squares

To make rows

Refer to Fig. 2 when arranging the fabric pieces in a row.

1. With right sides facing and raw edges aligned, stitch 1 large A triangle to 1 C square followed by another large A triangle as shown in the diagram.

2. Open seams and press.

3. With right sides facing and raw edges aligned, stitch a small A triangle to the top edge of the C portion of the A-C-A row. Open seams and press.

4. Continue to make rows in this way, following Fig. 3 for fabric arrangement. Row #10 begins and ends with a small triangle. You will have a total of 19 rows.

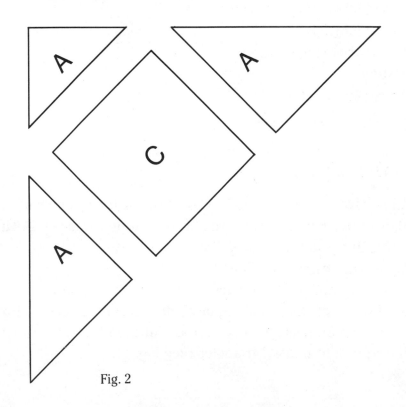

Fig. 2

Joining rows

1. Refer to Fig. 3 for row sequence.
2. With right sides facing and raw edges aligned, stitch the rows together along one long edge. Open seams and press.

Note: The 4 small triangles are located at each corner of the finished quilt top. There is a large triangle piece on either end of each row of squares.

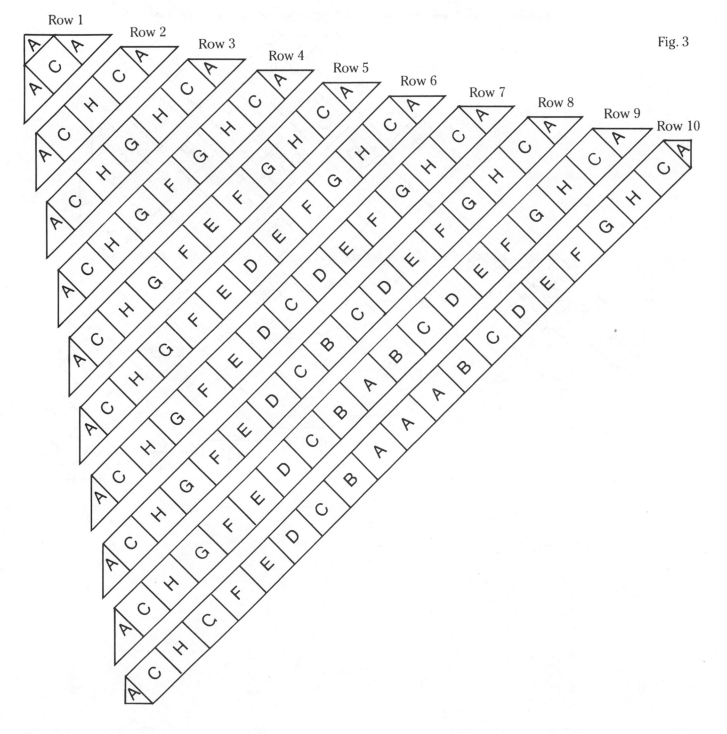

Fig. 3

Fig. 3

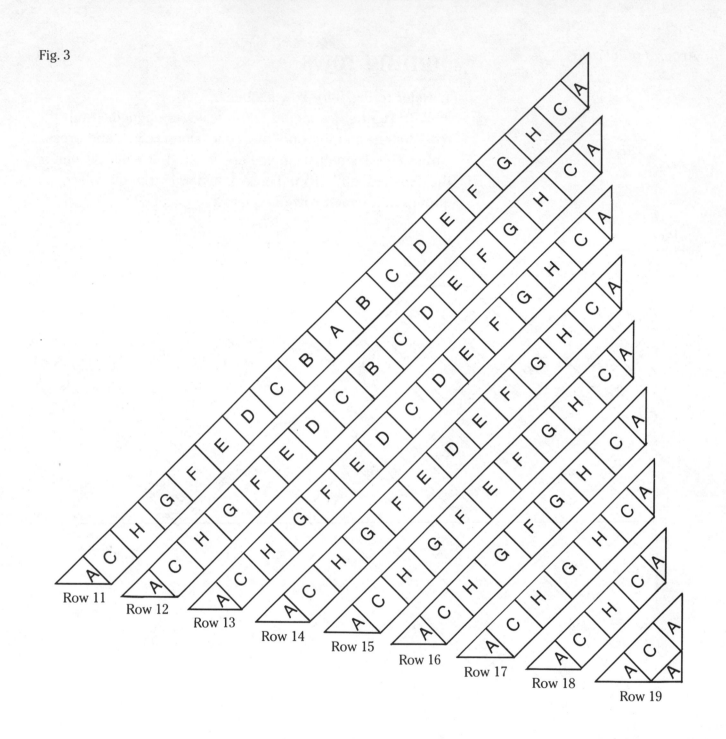

Row 11
Row 12
Row 13
Row 14
Row 15
Row 16
Row 17
Row 18
Row 19

70

Preparing the backing

1. Cut the batting ¼ inch smaller than the quilt top all around.
2. Cut the backing fabric in half so you have two pieces of 2 yards each.
3. With right sides facing and raw edges aligned, stitch these pieces together along one long edge to create the backing piece. Trim to quilt top size.
4. Baste the top, batting, and backing together with long stitches through all three layers. Begin at the center of the quilt and baste to each outer corner.
5. Pin and baste around the outside edges.

Quilting

1. To hand-quilt, begin at the center of the top and work outward taking small running stitches ¼ inch on both sides of each seam line. End the stitches ½ inch short of the outer edges.
2. To quilt by machine, stitch along the seam line of each square, taking care not to let the batting bunch up.

To finish

1. When all quilting is complete, clip the basting stitches away.
2. Fold the raw edges of the top and backing to the inside ¼ inch and press. Stitch around entire quilt to close. If hand-stitching, use a slipstitch.

Country Roads

The use of colors, especially the red accents, is what gives this quilted wallhanging its dynamic and directional quality. This is one of the few quilts in the book with lattice strips separating the squares. The directions of the squares must be done correctly to make this pattern work. Early folk quilters deliberately made an error in their quiltmaking to show the imperfection of the human being. This is not a good place to exercise this idea, however. Perfection is what makes this design work. The finished size is 52 × 52 inches.

Materials

(all fabric is 45 inches wide)
½ yard calico fabric A
1 yard solid color B
1 yard solid color C
1½ yards solid white D
2 yards solid blue E
3 yards backing fabric
batting
thread to match fabric colors
needle for hand-quilting
cardboard for template

Directions

(all pieces used for this quilt are rectangles)
A—32 strips 2½ × 5½ inches
B—32 strips 2½ × 9½ inches
C—32 strips 2½ × 13½ inches
D—16 strips 2½ × 15½ inches
The following E pieces are for the lattice strips:
12—2½ × 10½ inches
 3—2½ × 46½ inches
 2—3½ × 46½ inches
 2—3½ × 52½ inches

To make a block

1. Refer to Fig. 1. With right sides facing and raw edges aligned, center an A piece on a B piece and stitch together along one long raw edge.
2. Open seams and press.
3. Next, join a C piece, followed by a D piece, then C, B, and ending with an A piece joined as you did in the beginning.
4. Open all seams and press (see Fig. 2).

Fig. 1

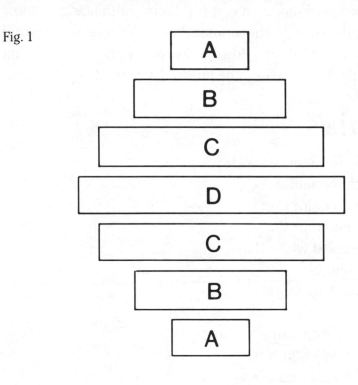

Fig. 2

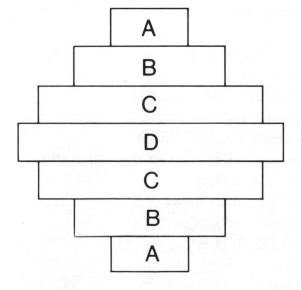

5. Using cardboard, mark and cut a square piece 10½ × 10½ inches to use as a template.

6. Refer to Fig. 3 and place the template on the fabric, being sure to center the corners as shown.

7. Mark around the template on the fabric and cut out. You will have a ¼-inch seam allowance. Make 16 blocks in this way (see Fig. 4).

Fig. 3

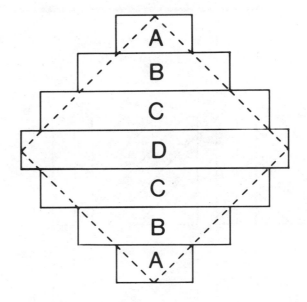

Fig. 4

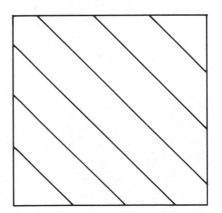

To make a row

1. With right sides facing and raw edges aligned, join a 2½ × 10½-inch lattice strip to one side of the first block as shown in Fig. 5.
2. Open seams and press.
3. As you add the blocks, notice that each is placed in a different direction in the row.
4. Continue to add 3 more blocks separated by lattice strips. Open all seams and press.
5. Make 4 rows in this way, always checking the diagram to be sure each block is placed correctly.

Fig. 5

Joining rows

1. With right sides facing and raw edges aligned, join a 2½ × 46½-inch lattice strip to the bottom long edge of the first row of blocks as per Fig. 6.
2. Open seams and press.
3. Continue to join the next 3 rows of blocks in this way. Each row is separated by a lattice strip. Open all seams and press.

Fig. 6

Joining borders

1. With right sides facing and raw edges aligned, join the last 2 lattice strips (3½ × 46½ inches) to the top and bottom rows of the quilt.

2. Open seams and press.

3. Next, join the long strips (3½ × 52½ inches) to each long side edge of the quilt top. Open seams and press (see Fig. 7).

Fig. 7

Preparing the backing

1. Cut the batting ¼ inch smaller than the quilt top all around.

2. Cut the backing fabric in half so you have two pieces 1½ yards each.

3. With right sides facing and raw edges aligned, stitch these pieces together along one long edge. Open seams and press.

4. Baste the top, batting, and backing together with long stitches through all three layers. Begin at the center of the quilt and baste to each outer corner.

5. Pin or baste around the outside edges.

Quilting

1. To hand-quilt, begin at the center of the top and work outward, taking small running stitches ¼ inch on both sides of each seam line. End the stitches ½ inch before the seam line at the edges of the quilt.

2. To quilt by machine, stitch along the seam line of each fabric piece (all strips that have been pieced together, including lattice strips).

To finish

1. When all quilting is complete, clip the basting stitches away.

2. Fold the raw edges of the top under ¼ inch and press. Turn the raw edges of the backing fabric to the inside and press.

3. Stitch the opening edges closed with a slipstitch, or machine-stitch all around.

Squares and Blocks

One color scheme is used for this quilt, but the variety of prints makes it seem colorful and lively. There is texture, which gives this quilt interest. Because the fabric manufacturers print many different patterns using variations of the same dye color, it is possible to coordinate a monochromatic scheme by adding variety and still maintain contrast with dark and light patterns. In this way you can choose the color of your room and find calicos, for example, in that color that all go together. For this type of quilt it is best to buy all your prints from the same manufacturer's line. This quilt measures 70 × 90 inches and will fit a double or queen-size bed.

Materials

(all fabric is 45 inches wide)
1 yard blue calico A
1 yard blue calico B
1 yard blue calico C
2 yards navy blue calico D
3 yards light blue calico E
5½ yards backing fabric
batting
thread to match fabric colors
needle for hand-quilting

Directions

Begin by cutting all fabric as follows:
A—2 strips 5½ × 45 inches
A—4 strips 3 × 45 inches
B—2 strips 5½ × 45 inches
B—4 strips 3 × 45 inches
C—2 strips 5½ × 45 inches
C—4 strips 3 × 45 inches
D—12 strips 3 × 45 inches
D—6 strips 5½ × 45 inches
E—31 squares 10½ × 10½ inches

Strip piecing for block #1

1. With right sides facing and raw edges aligned, stitch a 3 × 45-inch D strip to a 5½ × 45-inch A strip, along one long edge.

2. Open seams and press.

3. Next, join another 3 × 45-inch D strip in the same way. Open seams and press.

4. Cut the pieced strip into 3-inch segments as shown in Fig. 1. Make 28 segments.

5. With right sides facing and raw edges aligned, stitch a 3 × 45-inch A strip to a 5½ × 45-inch D strip along one long edge. Open seams and press.

6. Next, join another 3 × 45-inch A strip in the same way. Open seams and press.

7. Join 3 more strips in the same way and cut into 5½-inch segments as shown in Fig. 2. Make 14 segments.

8. With right sides facing and raw edges aligned, join segments to make a block. Refer to Fig. 3.

9. Open seams and press. Continue to join segments in this way to make 14 #1 blocks.

3½″   Fig. 1

| D |
| A |
| D |

5½″   Fig. 2

| A |
| D |
| A |

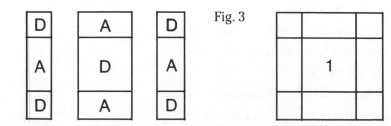

Fig. 3

Strip piecing for block #2

1. With right sides facing and raw edges aligned, stitch a 3 × 45-inch D strip to a 5½ × 45-inch B strip.

2. Open seams and press.

3. Next, join another D strip in the same way. Open seams and press.

4. Refer to Fig. 4 and cut pieced strips into 5½-inch segments. Make 18 segments.

5. With right sides facing and raw edges aligned, stitch a 3 × 45-inch B strip to a 5½ × 45-inch D strip along one long edge. Open seams and press.

6. Next, join another B strip in the same way. Open seams and press.

7. Cut into 5½-inch segments as shown in Fig. 5. Make 9.

8. With right sides facing and raw edges aligned, join segments to make a block. Refer to Fig. 6.

9. Open seams and press. Continue to join segments in this way to make 9 #2 blocks.

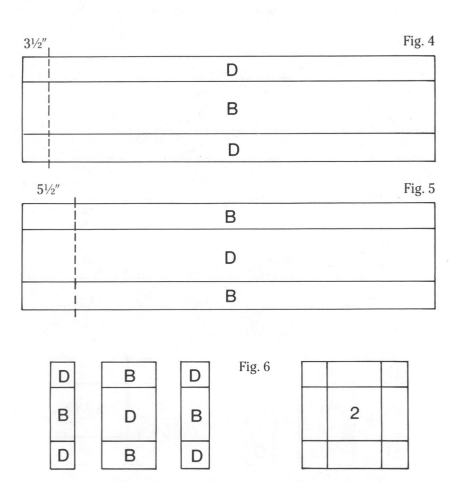

Strip piecing for block #3

1. With right sides facing and raw edges aligned, stitch a 3 × 45-inch D strip to a 5½ × 45-inch C strip, along one long edge.

2. Open seams and press.

3. Next, join another 5½ × 45-inch D strip in the same way. Open seams and press.

4. Cut the pieced strip into 3-inch segments as shown in Fig. 7. Make 18 segments.

5. With right sides facing and raw edges aligned, stitch a 3 × 45-inch C strip to a 5½ × 45-inch D strip along one long edge. Open seams and press.

6. Next join another 3 × 45-inch C strip in the same way. Open seams and press.

7. Cut into 5½-inch segments as shown in Fig. 8. Make 9.

8. With right sides facing and raw edges aligned, join segments together as shown in Fig. 9 to make a block.

9. Open seams and press. Continue to join segments in this way to make 9 #3 blocks.

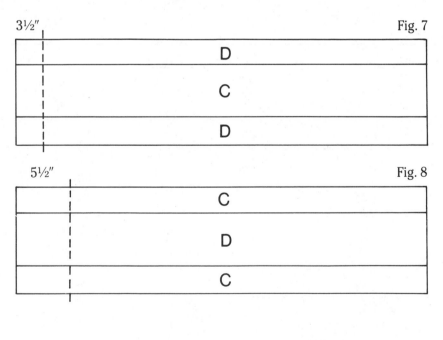

Fig. 7

Fig. 8

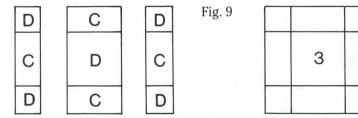

Fig. 9

To make rows

1. With right sides facing and raw edges aligned, stitch a #1 block to an E square along one edge.
2. Open seams and press.
3. Refer to Fig. 10 and continue to join a #2 block, followed by an E square, then a #3 block, an E square, and finally a #1 block.
4. Open all seams and press.
5. To make row #2, refer to Fig. 11. With right sides facing and raw edges aligned, stitch an E square to a #3 block along one long edge. Open seams and press.
6. Continue to add another E square, then a #1 block, an E square, a #2 block, and finally an E square.
7. Open all seams and press.
8. Continue to make rows by alternating row #1 and row #2 as shown in Fig. 12.

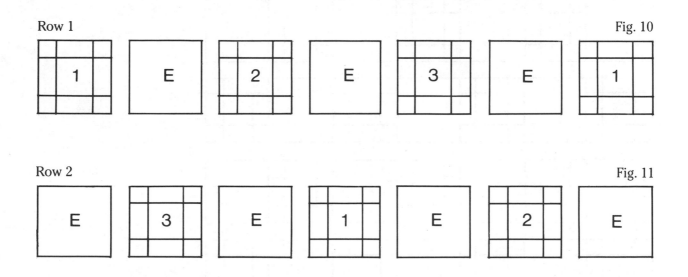

Row 1   Fig. 10

Row 2   Fig. 11

Joining rows

1. With right sides facing and raw edges aligned, join the first row to the second row along the bottom long edge.
2. Open seams and press.
3. Continue to join rows in the same way.
4. Open all seams and press (see Fig. 12).

Fig. 12

Preparing the backing

1. Cut the batting ½ inch smaller than the quilt top all around.
2. Cut the backing fabric in half so you have two pieces of 2¾ yards each.
3. With right sides facing and raw edges aligned, stitch these pieces together along one long edge to create the backing for the quilt top.
4. Trim to quilt top size.
5. Baste the top, batting, and backing together with long stitches through all three layers. Begin at the center of the quilt and baste to each outer corner.
6. Pin or baste around the outside edges.

Quilting

1. To hand-quilt, begin at the center of the top and work outward, taking small running stitches ¼ inch on both sides of each seam line. End stitches ½ inch from outer edges.
2. To quilt by machine, stitch along the seam line of each pieced square and inside the seam line of the E squares.

To finish

1. When all quilting is complete, clip the basting stitches away.
2. Fold the raw edges of the top under ¼ inch and press. Turn backing edges to inside ¼ inch and press.
3. Stitch together with a slipstitch, or machine-stitch all around outside edge.

Pinwheel

This quilt pattern takes its name from a child's pinwheel design, a familiar motif in American folk quilts. It is frequently made with red and white triangles for a dramatic effect, but this time I thought it might be nice to do something different.

The technique employs the quick cut-and-sew right triangle method, which makes it quite easy. The borders outline the center design and enable you to adjust the size. This was planned for a double or queen-size bed and is 70 × 84 inches.

Materials

(all fabric is 45 inches wide)
2 yards printed fabric A
2 yards solid fabric B
2½ yards printed fabric C
4 yards backing fabric
batting
thread to match fabric colors
needle for hand-quilting

Directions

1. Place fabric A face down and measure and mark off 40 squares 7 × 7 inches.
2. Next draw a diagonal line through each square to make 2 triangles.
3. With right sides facing, pin the marked fabric A to the solid fabric B.
4. Using the diagonal lines that you've just drawn as a guide, stitch ¼ inch on each side of this line. Refer to Fig. 1. You have just completed the first step in the easy cut-and stitch right triangle method.
5. Cut on all solid lines to create 80 squares of print and solid fabric triangles.

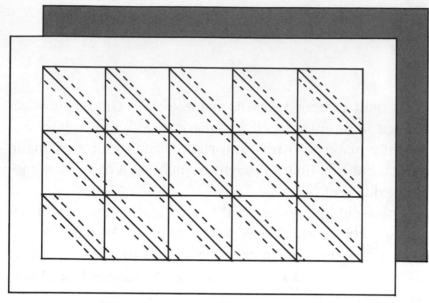

Fig. 1 Quick-and-Easy Triangle Method

To make a block

1. With right sides facing and raw edges aligned, stitch 2 fabric squares together as shown in Fig. 2

2. Attach 2 more squares together as shown in Fig. 2.

3. Open seams and press.

4. With right sides facing and raw edges aligned, stitch the 4 squares together to form a block. The fabric comes together to form a pinwheel design.

5. Continue to do this to make 20 blocks of 4 squares each.

Fig. 2

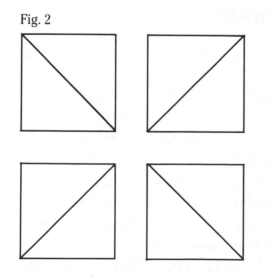

To make a row

1. With right sides facing and raw edges aligned, stitch 2 blocks together.
2. Open seams and press.
3. Repeat with 2 more blocks to make a row of 4.
4. Continue to make 5 rows (see Fig. 3).

Fig. 3

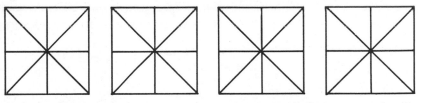

Joining rows

1. With right sides facing and raw edges aligned, stitch row #1 to row #2 along one long edge (see Fig. 4).
2. Open seams and press.
3. Repeat by joining row #3 to row #2 in the same way. Continue to join all rows in this way.
4. Open all seams and press.

Fig. 4

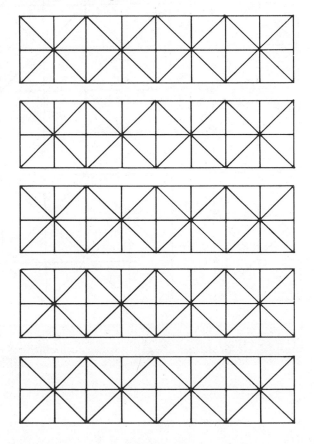

Making borders

1. Cut 2 fabric pieces C 2½ × 56½ inches for the top and bottom border strips.
2. Cut 2 fabric pieces C 2½ × 84½ inches for the side border pieces.
3. With right sides facing and raw edges aligned, stitch the top and bottom border strips to the quilt top.
4. Open seams and press.
5. Join the side border pieces to the quilt top in the same way (see Fig. 5).

Fig. 5

Preparing the backing

1. Cut the batting ¼ inch smaller than the quilt top all around.
2. Cut the backing fabric in half so you have two pieces 2 yards each.
3. With right sides facing and raw edges aligned, stitch these pieces together along one long edge to create the backing for the quilt top.
4. Baste the top, batting, and backing together with long stitches through all three layers. Begin at the center of the quilt and baste to each outer corner.
5. Pin or baste around the outside edges, if needed.

Quilting

1. To hand-quilt, begin at the center of the top and work outward, taking small running stitches ¼ inch on both sides of each seam line. End the stitches ½ inch before reaching outer edges.
2. To quilt by machine, stitch along all seam lines of each block and along the borders.

To finish

1. When all quilting is complete, clip the basting stitches away.
2. Fold the raw edges of the top under ¼ inch and press. Stitch together with a slipstitch, or machine-stitch all around.

Shadow Quilt

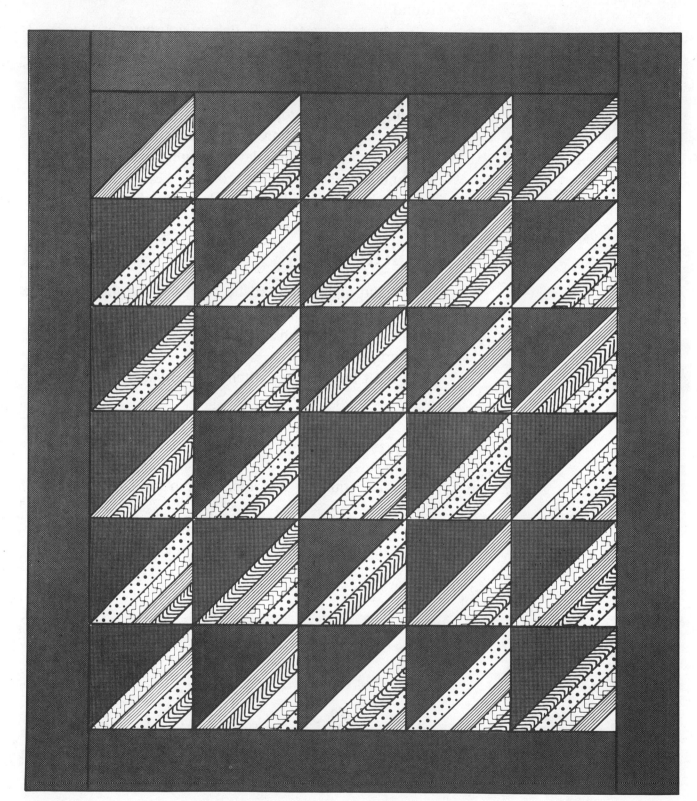

Often called Sunshine and Shadow, this is a popular Amish design. It can be created as a wallhanging or for any size bed without distorting the pattern. Half of each square is dark, the other half is light. This design is often done in black and muted earth tones or pastels for a dramatic effect of sunshine and shadows. Like many piecing projects, it looks more difficult than it is. The secret is the strip-cutting sewing method. The finished quilt is 66 × 76 inches and will fit a double or queen-size bed.

Materials

(all fabric is 45 inches wide)
1 yard light green solid fabric A
1 yard yellow solid fabric B
1 yard lavender solid fabric C
1 yard pink-and-white printed fabric D
1 yard light blue solid fabric E
3 yards royal blue fabric for borders
4½ yards backing fabric
batting
thread to match fabric colors
needle for hand-quilting

Directions

Begin by cutting all border pieces as follows:
2 pieces 8½ × 50½ inches for top and bottom
2 pieces 8½ × 76½ inches for the sides
From the remaining border fabric (royal blue) cut the following:
15 squares 11 × 11 inches
    Cut each square on the diagonal into 2 triangles each, making 30 triangles.
From each of the following cut 10 strips 2 × 32 inches:
Light green A
Yellow B
Lavender C
Pink/white D
Light blue E
1. With right sides facing and raw edges aligned, sew a green A strip to a yellow B strip along one long edge with a ¼-inch seam allowance.

2. Open seams and press.

3. Next, attach a C strip, followed by a D and ending with an E strip in the same way.

4. Open all seams and press.

5. Make 2 pieces with this sequence.

6. Make 2 pieces each in the following sequence.

B-C-D-E-A

C-D-E-A-B

D-E-A-B-C

E-A-B-C-D

7. Cut each piece into 3 triangles as shown in Fig. 1. You now have 6 triangles from each sequence for a total of 30 strip triangles.

Fig. 1

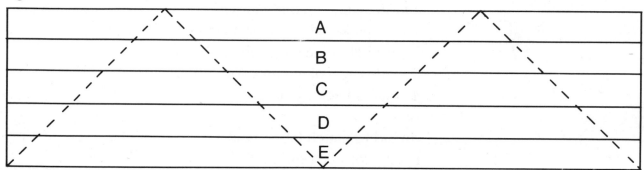

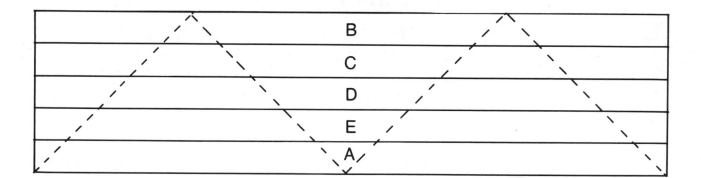

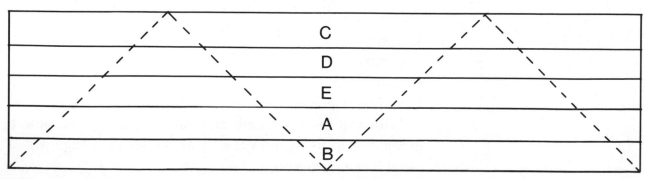

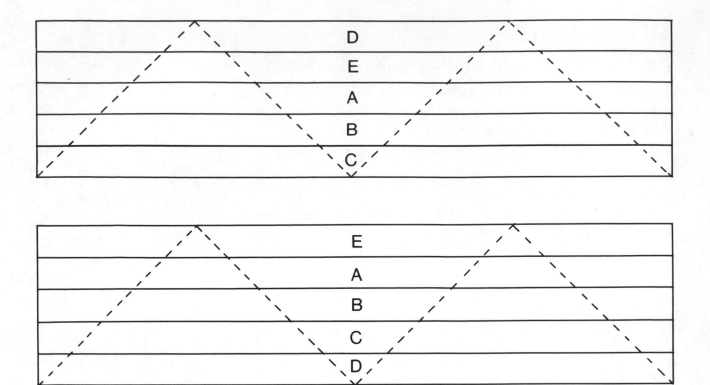

To make a block

1. With right sides facing and raw edges aligned, stitch 1 royal blue triangle to 1 strip triangle along the long edge as shown in Fig. 2.
2. Open seams and press.
3. Continue to do this to make 30 blocks. Open all seams and press.

Fig. 2

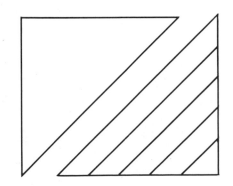 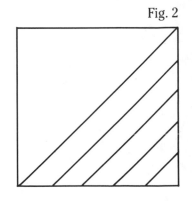

To make a row

1. You can make up a row using any combination of blocks that appeals to you, but it's a good idea to lay out all blocks before sewing. The layout should have the designs going in the same direction as shown in Fig. 3.

2. With right sides facing and raw edges aligned, stitch 2 blocks together along one edge.

3. Open seams and press.

4. Continue to join blocks until you have a horizontal row of 5 blocks. Open all seams and press.

5. Make 5 more rows.

Fig. 3

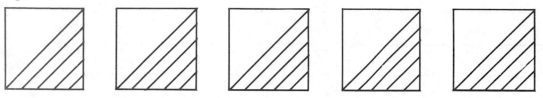

Joining rows

1. With right sides facing and raw edges aligned, join the first row to the second row along the bottom long edge.
2. Open seams and press.
3. Refer to Fig. 4 and continue to join the rows in the same way.
4. Open all seams and press.

Fig. 4

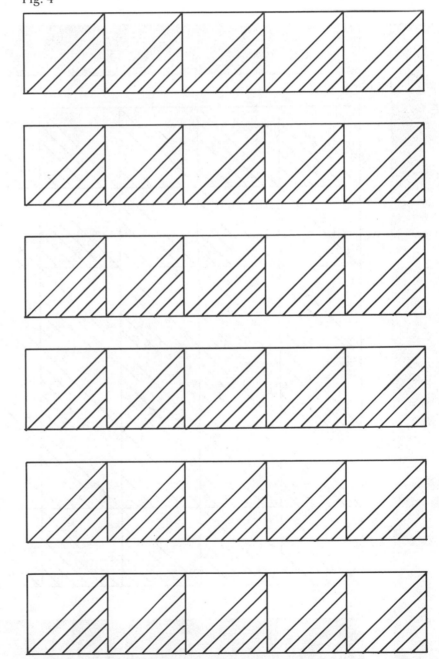

Joining borders

1. With right sides facing and raw edges aligned, join the top and bottom border pieces to the top of the quilt (see Fig. 5).
2. Open seams and press.
3. Join side border pieces in the same way. Open seams and press.

Fig. 5

Preparing the backing

1. Cut the batting ½ inch smaller than the quilt top all around.
2. Cut the backing fabric in half so you have two pieces of 2½ yards each.
3. With right sides facing and raw edges aligned, stitch these pieces together along one long edge to create the backing for the quilt top.
4. Trim to quilt top size.
5. Baste the top, batting, and backing together with long stitches through all three layers. Begin at the center of the quilt and baste to each outer corner.
6. Pin or baste around the outside edges.

Quilting

1. To hand-quilt, begin at the center of the top and work outward, taking small running stitches ¼ inch on both sides of each seam line. End the stitches ½ inch before the seam line at the edges of the quilt.
2. To quilt by machine, stitch along the seam line of each strip and join seams of each block, taking care that the batting does not bunch up.

To finish

1. When all quilting is complete, clip the basting stitches away.
2. Fold the raw edges of the top under ¼ inch and press. Turn backing edges to the inside ¼ inch and press.
3. Stitch together with a slipstitch, or machine-stitch all around.

Square Deal

This contemporary design is applied to a quilted wallhanging that is 70 × 70 inches. It would also look nice on a double bed. It is an interesting pattern made of red-and-white triangles surrounded by white with a blue border. The center is pieced and the quilting stitches continue the design into the surrounding white area.

This design uses a quick cut-and-sew right triangle technique, in which the result looks harder than it actually is.

Materials

(all fabric is 45 inches wide)
2 yards solid blue fabric A
2 yards solid rose fabric B
2½ yards white fabric C
4 yards backing fabric
batting
thread to match fabric colors
needle for hand-quilting
ruler
pencil

Directions

Begin by cutting all border pieces as follows:
A—2 pieces 1½ × 68½ inches
A—2 pieces 1½ × 70½ inches
B—2 pieces 6½ × 56½ inches
B—2 pieces 6½ × 68½ inches
C—2 pieces 12½ × 32½ inches
C—2 pieces 12½ × 56½ inches

Quick-and-easy triangle method

1. Using C fabric, measure and mark with a pencil 30 squares 5 × 5 inches on the wrong side of the fabric.
2. Draw a diagonal line from one corner to the other through each square.
3. With right sides facing and raw edges aligned, pin the penciled C fabric to a piece of A fabric cut to the same size.
4. Stitch ¼ inch on each side of the diagonal lines as shown in Fig. 1.

5. Cut on all solid lines. You will have 30 blue-and-white squares.

6. Using B fabric, measure and mark 2 squares 5 × 5 inches on the wrong side of the fabric.

7. Draw a diagonal line through the squares from one corner to the other.

8. With right sides facing and raw edges aligned, pin the penciled fabric to a piece of A fabric cut to the same size.

9. Stitch ¼ inch on each side of the diagonal lines. Cut on all solid lines. There should be 4 rose and blue squares.

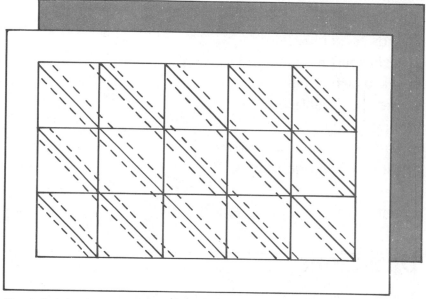

Fig. 1 Quick-and-Easy Triangle Method

To make a row

1. With right sides facing and raw edges aligned, join 2 squares along one edge as shown in Fig. 2.

2. Open seams and press.

3. Continue to join 2 more squares in this way. Open seams and press.

4. Note that the next 4 squares in the row are placed in the opposite direction. There are 8 squares in each row.

5. Open all seams and press.

6. Continue to make all rows according to the diagram (see Fig. 3).

Fig. 2

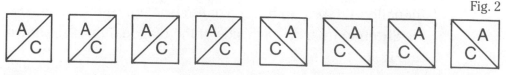

Joining rows

1. With right sides facing and raw edges aligned, stitch row #1 to row #2 along the bottom long edge.
2. Open seams and press.
3. Refer to Fig. 3 and continue to join all rows. Open all seams and press.

Fig. 3

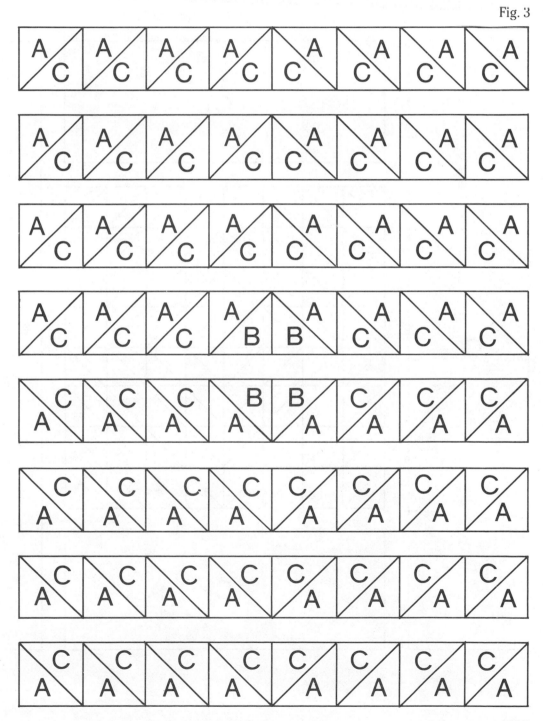

Joining borders

1. With right sides facing and raw edges aligned, join the top and bottom C pieces (12½ × 32½ inches) to the top and bottom of the quilt as shown in Fig. 4.
2. Open seams and press.
3. Join the side border C pieces (12½ × 56½ inches) in the same way. Open seams and press.

Fig. 4

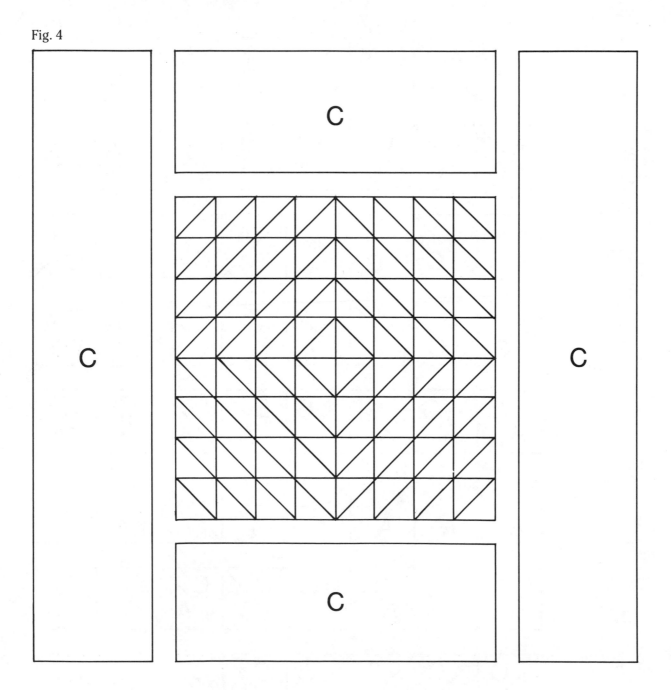

4. Next, join the top and bottom B pieces in the same way. Open seams and press (see Fig. 5).

5. Join the side border B pieces (6½ × 68½ inches) in the same way. Open seams and press.

6. Next, join A border pieces according to Fig. 5. Open seams and press.

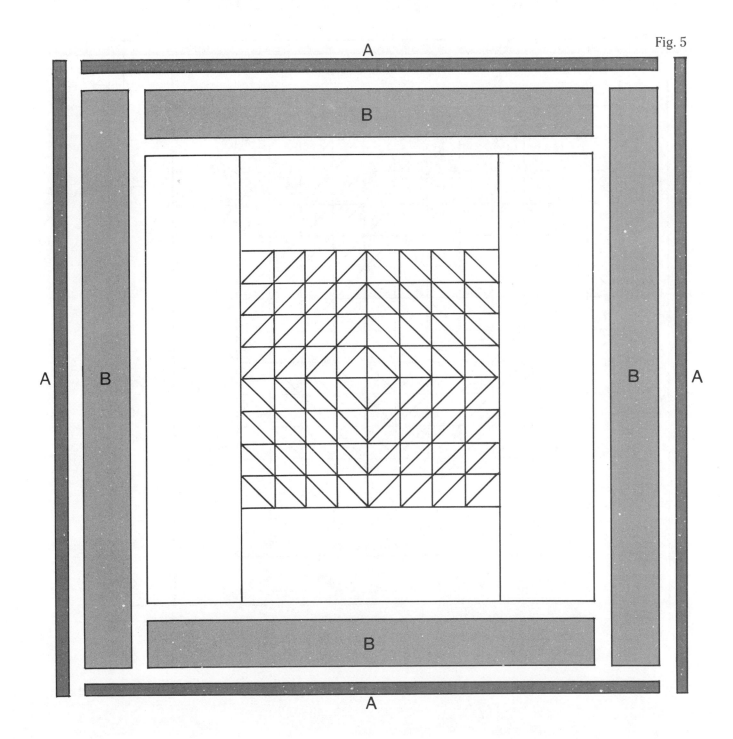

Fig. 5

Marking quilt pattern

1. Using a ruler and a pencil, extend all the pieced seam lines diagonally, horizontally, and vertically on the white border fabric.

2. Fill the entire area as shown in Fig. 6.

Fig. 6

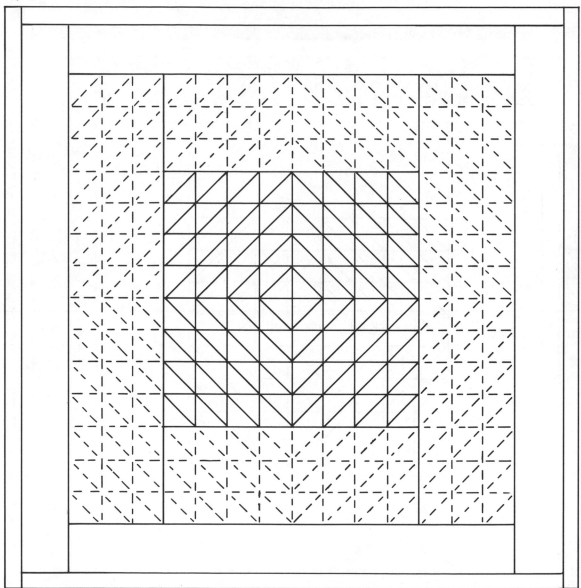

Preparing the backing

1. Cut the batting ½ inch smaller than the quilt top all around.
2. Cut the backing fabric in half so you have two pieces 2 yards each.
3. With right sides facing and raw edges aligned, stitch the 2 pieces together to create the backing for your quilt.
4. Trim to quilt top size.
5. Baste the top, batting, and backing together with long stitches through all three layers. Begin at the center of the quilt and baste to each outer corner.
6. Pin or baste around the outer edges.

Quilting

1. To hand-quilt, begin at the center of the top and work outward, taking small running stitches ¼ inch on both sides of each pieced seam line.
2. Stitch along all drawn lines on the white border area.
3. Take running stitches on either side of the border seams.
4. To machine-quilt, stitch along the seam lines of each pieced square, on the drawn quilting lines, and along all border seams.

To finish

1. When all quilting is complete, clip the basting stitches away.
2. Fold the raw edges of the top under ¼ inch and press. Turn backing edges to the inside ¼ inch and press.
3. Stitch around the outside edges with a slipstitch, or machine-stitch all around to close.

Crossroads

This is the only quilt in the book with a pattern piece. The bold black-and-red design creates an optical illusion when finished. All sewn lines are straight, but the squares don't always look parallel, which gives it an interesting quality. The geometric pattern is very contemporary, but this is essentially a traditional patchwork quilt. The finished size is 58 × 86 inches and would be perfect for a twin-size bed in a boy's room.

Materials

(all fabric is 45 inches wide)
1½ yards white fabric A
2½ yards red calico B
3 yards black calico C
3½ yards fabric for backing
batting
thread to match fabric colors
needle for hand-quilting
cardboard for template
tracing paper

Directions

1. Trace the pattern piece. Place this face down on the cardboard and rub over the traced lines. The outline will come off on the cardboard. Retrace over the lines to delineate more clearly.

2. Cut out the design outline from the cardboard.

3. Cut all fabric pieces as follows:

Red border B—2 pieces 2½ × 42½ inches for top and bottom
    2 pieces 2½ × 74½ inches for sides

Black border C—2 pieces 6½ × 46½ inches for top and bottom
    2 pieces 6½ × 86½ inches for sides

Blocks B—30 squares 6 × 6 inches
    Cut each square into 2 triangles each.

Blocks C—30 squares 6 × 6 inches
    Cut each square into 2 triangles.

Pattern A—60 pieces using the template, which allows for a ¼-inch seam allowance.

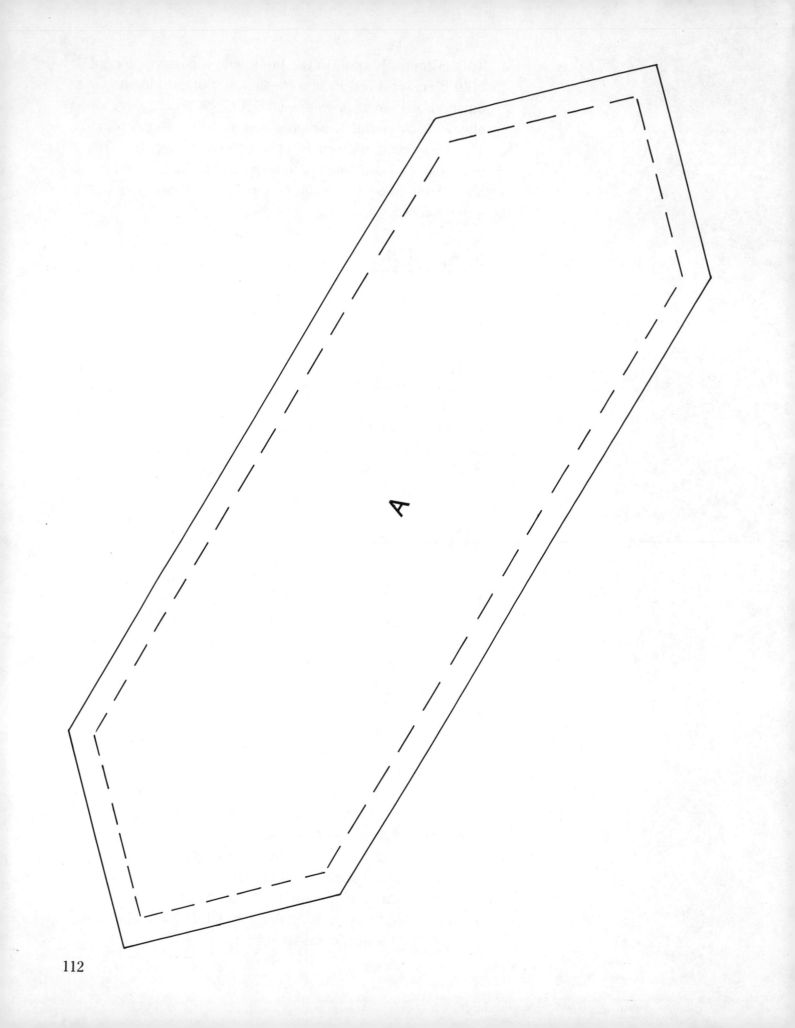

A

To make a block

1. With right sides facing and raw edges aligned, here stitch a red B triangle to a white A piece along the long edge as shown in Fig. 1.

2. Open seams and press.

3. Next, stitch a black C triangle to the other edge of the white A piece as shown in Fig. 1.

4. Open seams and press. You now have a square 7½ × 7½ inches.

5. Continue to make 60 blocks in this way. Open all seams and press.

Fig. 1

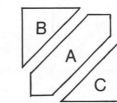

To make rows

1. Arrange 6 blocks in a horizontal row as shown in Fig. 2.

2. With right sides facing and raw edges aligned, stitch the first and second blocks together.

3. Open seams and press.

4. Continue to join all 6 blocks in this way. Open all seams and press.

5. Arrange 6 blocks in a horizontal row as shown in Fig. 3. Join together as you did for the first row.

6. Continue to join blocks, alternating the arrangement in each row, until you have made 10 rows of 6 blocks each (see Fig. 4).

7. Open all seams and press.

Fig. 2

Fig. 3

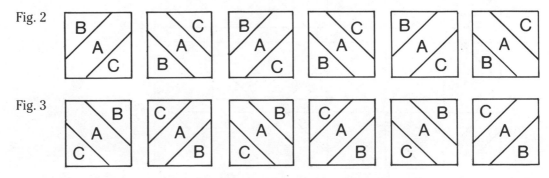

Joining rows

1. With right sides facing and raw edges aligned, join the first row to the second row along the bottom long edge.
2. Open seams and press.
3. Continue to join all 10 rows in this way. Open seams and press.

Fig. 4

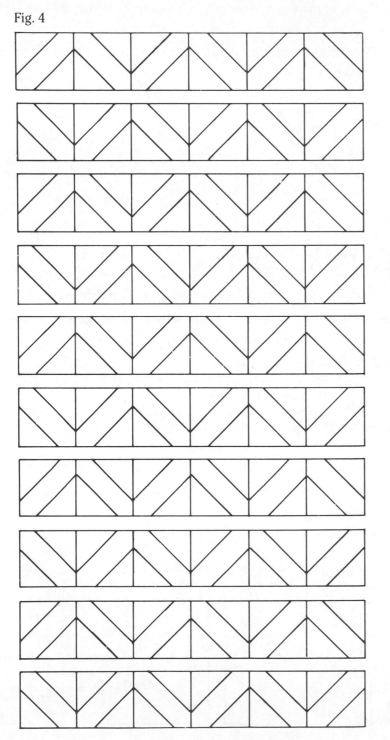

Joining borders

1. With right sides facing and raw edges aligned, stitch the top and bottom border B pieces (2½ × 42½ inches) to the top and bottom of the quilt as shown in Fig. 5.
2. Open seams and press.
3. Join side border B pieces (2½ × 74½ inches) in the same way. Open seams and press.
4. With right sides facing and raw edges aligned, join the top and bottom border C pieces (6½ × 46½ inches) to the top and bottom of the quilt (see Fig. 5).
5. Open seams and press.
6. Join side border C pieces in the same way. Open seams and press.

Fig. 5

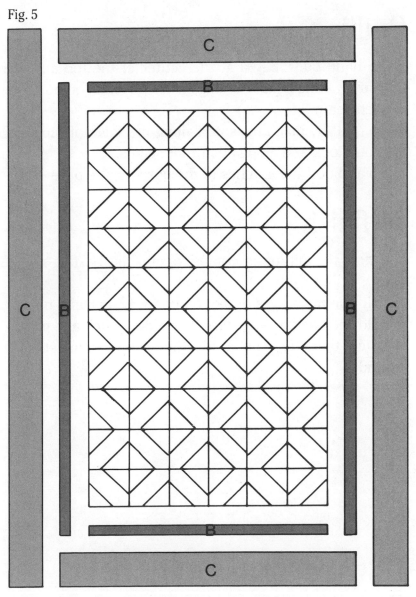

Preparing the backing

1. Cut the batting ½ inch smaller than the quilt top all around.
2. Cut the backing fabric in half so you have two pieces 1¾ yards each.
3. With right sides facing and raw edges aligned, stitch these pieces together along one long edge to create the backing for the quilt top.
4. Trim to quilt top size.
5. Baste the top, batting, and backing together with long stitches through all three layers. Begin at the center of the quilt and baste to each outer corner.
6. Pin or baste around the outside edges.

Quilting

1. To hand-quilt, begin at the center of the top and work outward, taking small running stitches ¼ inch on both sides of each seam line.
2. To quilt by machine, stitch along the seam of each piece of each block and along all border seams.
3. To add quilting stitches to the borders, see page 21.

To finish

1. When all quilting is complete, clip the basting stitches away.
2. Fold the raw edges of the top under ¼ inch and press.
3. Fold the backing edges to the inside ¼ inch and press.
4. Stitch together with a slipstitch, or machine-stitch all around.

Quilting pattern for Crossroads

Flying Geese

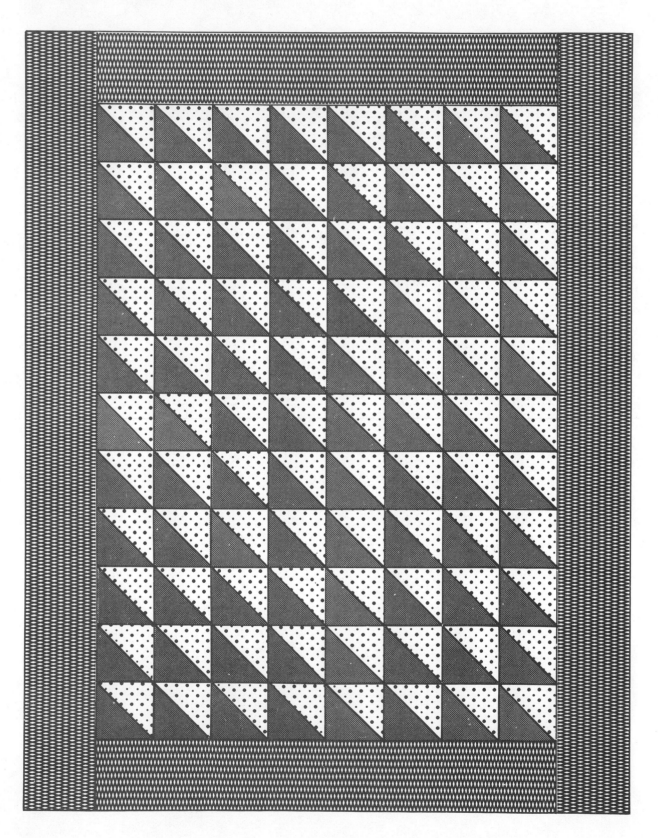

This quilt is made from many different scrap fabrics. Often the design is created with just two colors, such as black and white or red and white, for a dramatic effect. Whatever colors you use, the pattern should be made up of light and dark triangles. When cutting the triangles, it will save you a lot of time if you keep all the dark fabrics in one box and the lights in another. The finished quilt is 64 × 82 inches, which will fit a double or queen-size bed.

Materials

(all fabric is 45 inches wide)
½ yard each of 10 light fabrics A
½ yard each of 10 dark fabrics B
2½ yards dark print for borders
4 yards backing fabric
batting
thread to match fabric colors
needle for hand-quilting

Directions

1. Cut all light fabric A into 7 × 7-inch squares.
2. Cut each square on the diagonal so you have 2 triangles from each square. You will need 88 light triangles.
3. Cut all dark fabric B into 7 × 7-inch squares.
4. Cut each square on the diagonal so you have 2 triangles from each square. You will need 88 dark triangles.
5. With right sides facing and raw edges aligned, stitch a light triangle to a dark triangle along the long edge (see Fig. 1). You can mix the light and dark triangles any way you wish.
6. Open seams and press. Make 88 squares in this way.

Fig. 1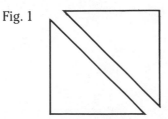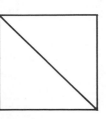

To make a row

Refer to Fig. 2 when joining squares to make a row.

1. With right sides facing and raw edges aligned, stitch 2 squares together along one edge as shown.

2. Open seams and press.

3. Continue to join squares in this way to make a horizontal row of 8 squares. The dark part of each square must always be on the left. Open seams and press.

5. Make 11 rows in this way.

Fig. 2

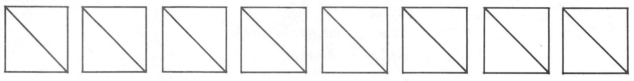

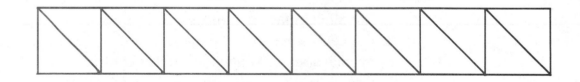

Joining rows

1. With right sides facing and raw edges aligned, stitch row #1 to row #2 along one long edge as shown in Fig. 3.

2. Open seams and press.

3. Repeat by joining row #3 to row #2 in the same way. Continue to join all rows in this way.

4. Open all seams and press.

Fig. 3

Making borders

Refer to Fig. 4.

1. Cut 2 fabric pieces 8½ × 48½ inches for the top and bottom border strips.

2. Cut 2 fabric pieces 8½ × 82½ inches for the side border pieces.

3. With right sides facing and raw edges aligned, stitch the top and bottom border strips to the quilt top.

4. Open seams and press.

5. Join the side border pieces to the quilt top in the same way. Open seams and press.

Fig. 4

Preparing the backing

1. Cut the batting ¼ inch smaller than the quilt top all around.
2. Cut the backing fabric in half so you have two pieces 2 yards each.
3. With right sides facing and raw edges aligned, stitch these pieces together along one long edge to create the backing for the quilt top.
4. Trim the fabric to match the quilt top.
5. Baste the top, batting, and backing together with long stitches through all three layers. Begin at the center of the quilt and baste to each outer corner.
6. Pin or baste around the outside edges, if needed.

Quilting

1. To hand-quilt, begin at the center of the top and work outward, taking small running stitches ¼ inch on both sides of each seam line. End the stitches ½ inch from the outer edges.
2. To quilt by machine, stitch along all seam lines of each triangle and along the borders.
3. You might want to quilt the borders as well. Refer to page 21 for directions.

To finish

1. When all quilting is complete, clip the basting stitches away.
2. Fold the raw edges of the top under ¼ inch and press. Stitch together with a slipstitch, or machine-stitch all around.

Harlequin

This design is made of scrap fabric pieces in alternating blocks of dark and light colors. It's a very busy quilt, as a variety of fabrics is used to make each block. The fabric can be placed at random, but for a simpler version you might select two colors in light and dark, such as red and white. This will make your cutting and piecing very easy and less time-consuming. But for economy's sake, a lot of leftover fabric can be put to good use here. The finished size is 56 × 72 inches, which will fit the top of a double bed.

Materials

(all fabric is 45 inches wide)
1 yard blue fabric A
1 yard gray fabric B
½ yard lavender fabric C
½ yard pink fabric D
½ yard yellow fabric E
½ yard pale blue fabric F
½ yard pale green fabric G
½ yard peach fabric H
3½ yards backing fabric
batting
thread to match fabric colors
needle for hand-quilting

Directions

Begin by cutting all fabric as follows:
A—63 squares 5 × 5 inches
    Cut each square into 2 triangles.
B—63 squares 5 × 5 inches
    Cut each square into 2 triangles.
Cut 21 squares 5 × 5 inches from each of the following fabrics: C, D, E, F, G, and H.
Cut each square into 2 triangles for a total of 42 triangles in each color.
1. With right sides facing and raw edges aligned, stitch an A triangle to a C triangle along the long edge (see Fig. 1).
2. Open seams and press. Make 21 of these squares.

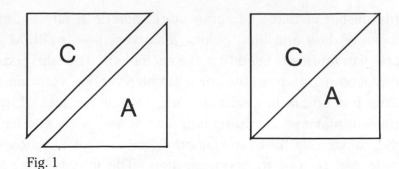

Fig. 1

3. Continue to join triangles in this way. The following indicates which pieces to join in order to make up the first set of squares:

D and A = make 21

E and A = make 21

F and A = make 21

G and A = make 21

H and A = make 21

4. Continue to join triangles to make up the following combinations for the second set of squares:

C and B = make 21

D and B = make 21

E and B = make 21

F and B = make 21

G and B = make 21

H and B = make 21

5. You have just finished the second set of squares. Open all seams and press.

To make a block

1. With right sides facing and raw edges aligned, stitch 2 squares together so that an A and a B triangle are joined along one edge (see Fig. 2).

2. Open seams and press.

3. Next, join 2 more squares so that a B and an A triangle are joined along one edge.

4. Open seams and press.

5. With right sides facing and raw edges aligned, stitch the 4 squares together along one long edge as shown in Fig. 2.

6. Open all seams and press.

7. You have completed one block. Make 63 squares in this way.

Harlequin

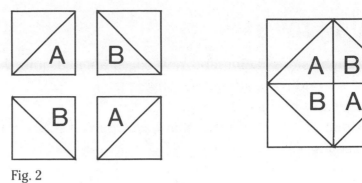

Fig. 2

To make a row

1. With right sides facing and raw edges aligned, stitch 2 blocks together along one long edge.
2. Open seams and press.
3. Continue to join blocks as shown in Fig. 3 to form a row of 7 blocks.
4. Open all seams and press.
5. Make 9 rows of 7 blocks each. Open all seams and press.

Fig. 3

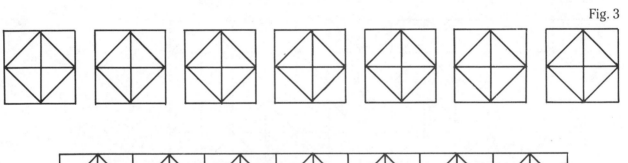

Joining rows

1. With right sides facing and raw edges aligned, join the first and second rows along one long edge.
2. Open seams and press.
3. Continue to join all rows in this way. Open all seams and press (see Fig. 4).

Fig. 4

Preparing the backing

1. Cut the batting ½ inch smaller than the quilt top all around.

2. Cut the backing fabric in half so you have two pieces 1¾ yards each.

3. With right sides facing and raw edges aligned, stitch these pieces together along the long edge.

4. Trim to fit quilt top, if necessary.

5. Baste the top, batting, and backing together with long stitches through all three layers. Begin at the center of the quilt and baste to each outer corner.

6. Pin or baste around outside edges.

Quilting

1. To hand-quilt, begin at the center of the top and work outward, taking small running stitches ¼ inch on both sides of the seam lines of each triangle piece.

2. To quilt by machine, stitch along the seam lines of each piece.

To finish

1. When all quilting is complete, clip the basting stitches away.

2. Fold the raw edges of the quilt under ¼ inch and press. Turn backing edges to the inside ¼ inch and press.

3. Stitch together with a slipstitch, or machine-stitch all around.

Spinning Spools

This vibrant, colorful quilt is a wonderful place to use all your fabric scraps. The placement of each spool creates a tumbling or spinning effect that is at once playful and active. The finished size is 66 × 77 inches, which fits a double bed. This quilt would also make a nice wallhanging or coverlet for a twin bed in a young person's room. Simply adjust the border or eliminate a row of blocks.

Materials

(all fabric is 45 inches wide)
½ yard light green fabric A
½ yard violet print B
½ yard yellow fabric C
½ yard red print D
½ yard pink fabric E
½ yard turquoise print F
½ yard light blue fabric G
½ yard red print H
3 yards blue print I
4 yards backing fabric
batting
thread to match fabric colors
needle for hand-quilting

Directions

Begin by cutting the fabric as follows:
A—10 squares 4½ × 4½ inches
A—5 squares 5 × 5 inches
    Cut each of the 5 squares into 2 triangles for a total of 10 triangles.
B—5 squares 5 × 5 inches
    Cut each square into 2 triangles each for a total of 10 triangles.
C—10 squares 4½ × 4½ inches
C—5 squares 5 × 5 inches
    Cut each of the 5 squares into 2 triangles for a total of 10 triangles.
D—5 squares 5 × 5 inches
    Cut each square into 2 triangles for a total of 10 triangles.

E—10 squares 4½ × 4½ inches

E—5 squares 5 × 5 inches

    Cut each of the 5 squares into 2 triangles for a total of 10 triangles.

F—5 squares 5 × 5 inches

    Cut each square into 2 triangles for a total of 10 triangles.

G—10 squares 4½ × 4½ inches

G—5 squares 5 × 5 inches

    Cut each of the 5 squares into 2 triangles for a total of 10 triangles.

H—5 squares 5 × 5 inches

    Cut each square into 2 triangles for a total of 10 triangles.

I—2 side border pieces 11½ × 77½ inches

I—2 top and bottom pieces 11½ × 44½ inches

I—12 squares 8½ × 8½ inches

I—7 squares 9 × 9 inches

    Cut the 7 squares into 2 triangles each for a total of 14 triangles.

I—1 square 9 × 9 inches

    Cut the 1 square into 4 small triangles.

To make block #1

1. With right sides facing and raw edges aligned, stitch an A triangle to a B triangle along the long edge as shown in Fig. 1. Make 5 of these squares.

2. Open seams and press.

3. With right sides facing and raw edges aligned, stitch the AB square to a solid A square along one edge as shown in Fig. 2. Open seams and press.

4. Next stitch a solid A square to a BA square in the same way. Open seams and press.

5. With right sides facing and raw edges aligned, stitch the 4 squares together along one long edge as shown in Fig. 3. Open seams and press.

6. You have just completed block #1 (see Fig. 4). Make 5 more blocks.

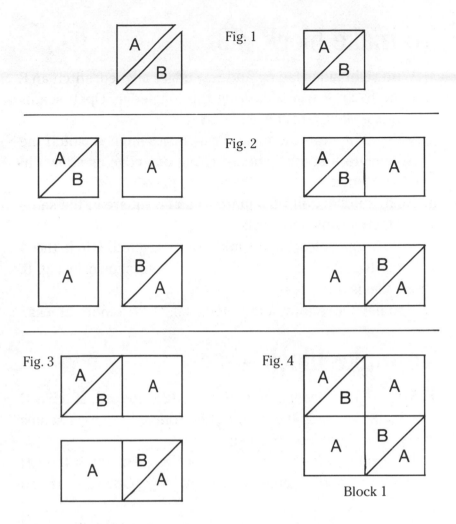

Fig. 1

Fig. 2

Fig. 3

Fig. 4

Block 1

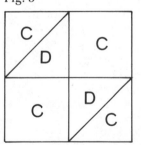

Fig. 5

Block 2

To make block #2

1. With right sides facing and raw edges aligned, stitch a C triangle to a D triangle along the long edge. Make 5 of these squares.

2. Open seams and press.

3. With right sides facing and raw edges aligned, stitch the CD square to a solid C square along one edge as shown in Fig. 2 for block #1.

4. Open seams and press.

5. Next, stitch a solid C square to a DC square in the same way. Open seams and press.

6. With right sides facing and raw edges aligned, stitch the 4 squares together along one long edge as shown in Fig. 3 for block #1. Open seams and press.

7. You have just completed block #2 (see Fig. 5). Make 5 more blocks.

To make block #3

1. With right sides facing and raw edges aligned, stitch an E triangle to an F triangle along the long edge. Open seams and press. Make 5 of these squares.
2. With right sides facing and raw edges aligned, stitch the EF square to a solid E square along one edge as shown in Fig. 2 for block #1. Open seams and press.
3. Next, stitch a solid E square to an FE square in the same way. Open seams and press.
4. With right sides facing and edges aligned, stitch the 4 squares together along one long edge as shown in Fig. 6. Open seams and press.
5. You have just completed block #3. Make 5 more blocks.

Fig. 6

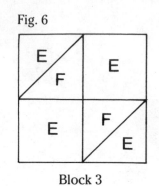

Block 3

To make block #4

1. With right sides facing and raw edges aligned, stitch a G triangle to an H triangle along the long edge. Open seams and press. Make 5 of these squares.
2. With right sides facing and edges aligned, stitch the GH square to a solid G square along one edge. Open seams and press.
3. Next, stitch a solid G square to an HG square in the same way. Open seams and press.
4. With right sides facing and edges aligned, stitch the 4 squares together along one long edge. Open seams and press (see Fig. 7).
5. You have now completed block #4. Make 5 of these blocks.

Fig. 7

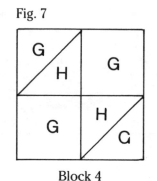

Block 4

To make rows

1. It is important to refer to Fig. 8 when assembling and joining blocks to make up the rows. **Note:** blocks #1 and #3 are turned in one direction, while blocks #2 and #4 are turned in the opposite direction. All pieced blocks are separated by a solid I square. Each row begins and ends with a large I triangle. A small I triangle is at each corner of the quilt top.

2. With right sides facing and raw edges aligned, stitch a large I triangle to a block #1 along one edge as shown in Fig. 8. Open seams and press.

3. Next, join another I triangle to the other edge of block #1. Open seams and press.

4. Continue to join blocks, squares, and triangles according to Fig. 8 until you have 8 rows. Open all seams and press.

Fig. 8

Joining rows

1. With right sides facing and raw edges aligned, stitch a small I triangle to the top of block #1 of the first row. Open seams and press.
2. Refer to Fig. 9 and join all rows in this way.
3. Open all seams and press.

Fig. 9

Row 1

Row 2

Row 3

Row 4

Row 5

Row 6

Row 7

Row 8

Joining borders

1. With right sides facing and raw edges aligned, stitch the top and bottom border I pieces (11½ × 44½ inches) to the top and bottom edges of the quilt top (see Fig. 10).
2. Open seams and press.
3. Join side border I pieces in the same way. Open seams and press.

Fig. 10

Preparing the backing

1. Cut the batting ½ inch smaller than the quilt top all around.
2. Cut the backing fabric in half so you have two pieces 2 yards each.
3. With right sides facing and raw edges aligned, stitch these pieces together along one long edge to create the backing for the quilt top.
4. Trim to size, if necessary.
5. Baste the top, batting, and backing together with long stitches through all three layers. Begin at the center of the quilt and baste to each outer corner.
6. Pin or baste around outside edges.

Quilting

1. To hand-quilt, begin at the center of the top and work outward, taking small running stitches ¼ inch on both sides of the seam lines of each patched piece.
2. Stitch around the seam line of each solid square.
3. To quilt by machine, stitch along the seam line of each piece and the joining seams of each border strip.
4. To add quilting stitches to the borders, see page 21.

To finish

1. When all quilting is complete, clip the basting stitches away.
2. Fold the raw edges of the top under ¼ inch and press. Turn backing edges to the inside ¼ inch and press.
3. Stitch together with a slipstitch, or machine-stitch all around.

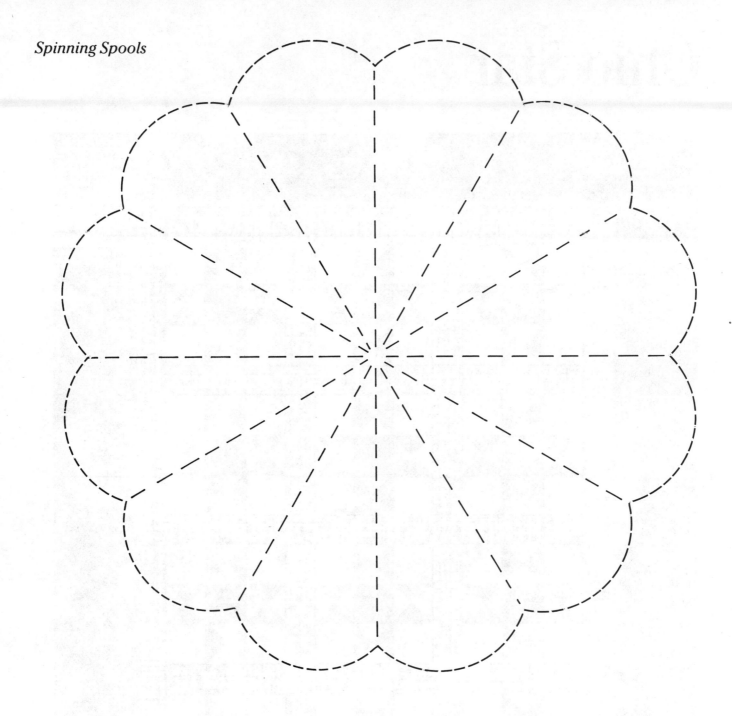

Quilting pattern for Spinning Spools

Ohio Star

This is one of the hardest quilts to do because you are combining squares and triangles. As with all patchwork, however, you are building one piece at a time. Once you have the basic design down, it's just a matter of repeating it.

Traditional colors in calico prints were used for this traditional design. If you follow the directions for easy cutting, it won't be difficult to make this popular quilt. The finished size is 68 × 84 inches, which will fit a double bed.

Materials

(all fabric is 45 inches wide)
1½ yard white fabric A
2 yards green calico B
2½ yards red calico C
4 yards backing fabric
batting
thread to match fabric colors
needle for hand-quilting

Directions

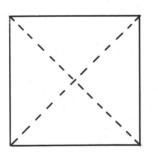

Fig. 1

Begin by cutting the fabric as follows:
A—48 squares 4½ × 4½ inches
A—24 squares 5½ × 5½ inches
    Cut the 24 squares on the diagonal so you have 4 triangles for each square for a total of 96 white triangles (see Fig. 1).
B—2 pieces 4½ × 68½ inches for side borders
B—5 pieces 4½ × 44½ inches for top, middle, and bottom strips
B—8 pieces 4½ × 12½ inches for lattice strips
C—2 pieces 8½ × 84½ inches for side borders
C—2 pieces 8½ × 52½ inches for top and bottom borders
C—12 squares 4½ × 4½ inches
C—24 squares 5½ × 5½ inches
    Cut each of the 24 squares into 4 triangles each as you did with the white squares. You will have a total of 96 red calico triangles (see Fig. 1).
1. With right sides facing and raw edges aligned, stitch a C and A triangle together along one long edge as shown in Fig. 2.

2. Open seams and press.

3. Repeat to make 96 red-and-white triangles.

4. Open all seams and press.

5. With right sides facing and raw edges aligned, stitch 2 of these triangles together along the long edge to make a square as shown in Fig. 3.

6. Open seams and press.

7. Make 48 squares in this way. Open all seams and press.

Fig. 2

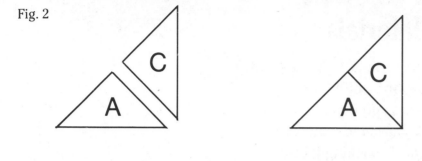

Fig. 3

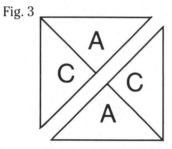

To make a block

Each block is made up of 9 squares. In order to refer to the piecing we will use the following letters to signify the squares:

A = a white square

B = a square made up of red-and-white triangles

C = a red square

1. With right sides facing and raw edges aligned, stitch an A square to a B square along one edge.

2. Open seams and press.

3. Join another A square to the B square as shown in Fig. 4. Open seams and press.

4. Next, join a B square to a C square, followed by another B square. Open seams and press.

5. Make another row of an A square stitched to a B square, followed by an A square for the third row.

6. Open all seams and press.

142

7. With right sides facing and raw edges aligned, stitch row #1 to row #2 along one long edge.

8. Open seams and press.

9. Join the third row in the same way. Open seams and press. You have completed a 9-square block (see Fig. 5). Continue until you have made 12 blocks in this way.

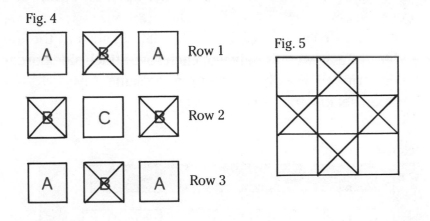

Fig. 4

Row 1

Row 2

Row 3

Fig. 5

To make a row

1. With right sides facing and raw edges aligned, stitch a block to one green 4½ × 12½-inch lattice strip as shown in Fig. 6.

2. Open seams and press.

3. Continue to join another block and lattice strip, ending with another block. Open seams and press.

4. Make 4 rows in this way. Open all seams and press.

Fig. 6

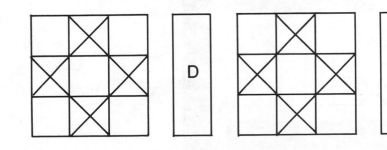

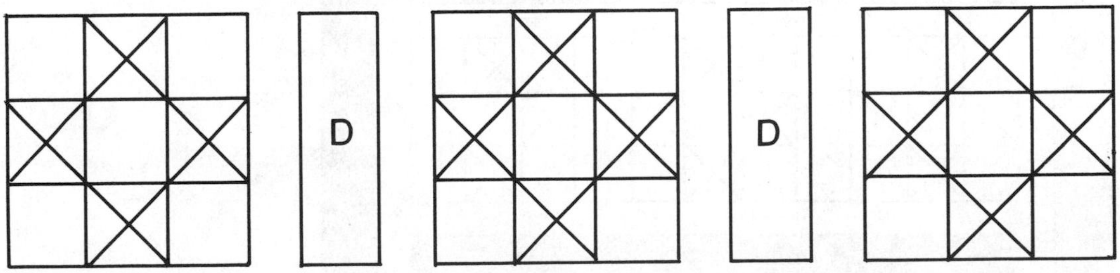

Joining rows

1. With right sides facing and raw edges aligned, stitch a green 4½ × 44½-inch lattice strip to a row of blocks along one long edge (see Fig. 7).
2. Open seams and press.
3. Continue to join rows in this way. Open all seams and press.
4. When all rows are joined, with a lattice strip at the top and bottom as well as between each row, attach side border green strips (4½ × 68½ inches) in the same way.
5. Open seams and press.

Fig. 7

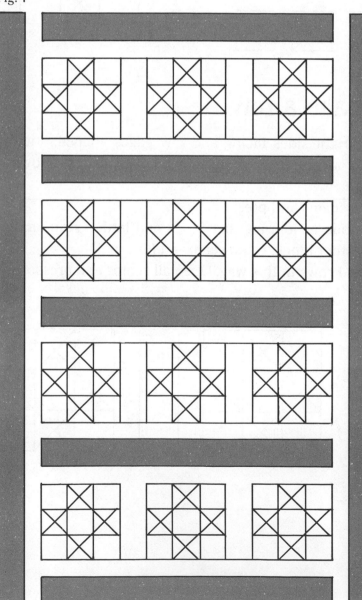

Joining borders

1. With right sides facing and raw edges aligned, stitch the top and bottom red 8½ × 52½-inch border strips to the quilt top (see Fig. 8).
2. Open seams and press.
3. Next, attach the side border red pieces (8½ × 84½ inches) in the same way. Open all seams and press.

Fig. 8

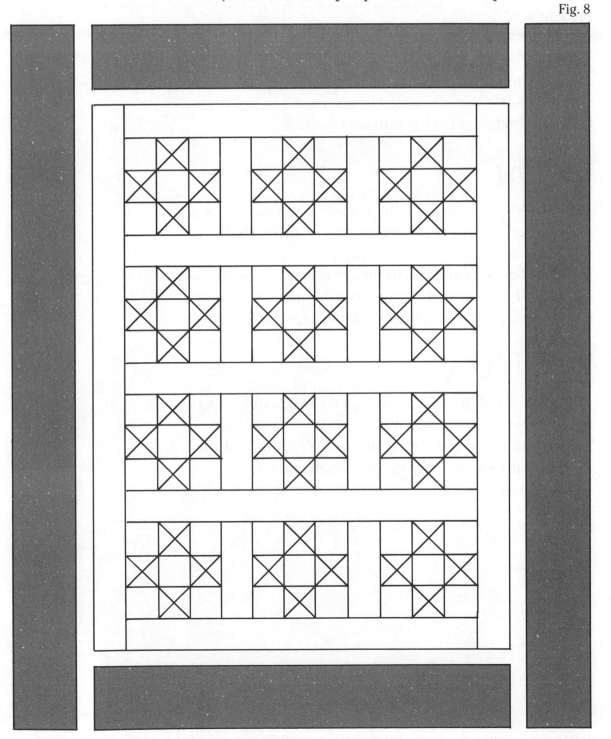

Preparing the backing

1. Cut the batting ½ inch smaller than the quilt top all around.
2. Cut the backing fabric in half so you have two pieces 2 yards each.
3. With right sides facing and raw edges aligned, stitch these pieces together along one long edge to create the backing for the quilt top.
4. Trim to quilt top size.
5. Baste the top, batting, and backing together with long stitches through all three layers. Begin at the center of the quilt and baste to each outer corner.
6. Pin or baste around the outside edges.

Quilting

1. To hand-quilt, begin at the center of the top and work outward, taking small running stitches ¼ inch on both sides of each seam line.
2. To add quilting stitches to the borders, see page 21.
3. To quilt by machine, stitch along the seam line of each pieced triangle and square, and all border and lattice seams.

To finish

1. When all quilting is complete, clip the basting stitches away.
2. Fold the raw edges of the top under ¼ inch and press. Turn backing edges to the inside ¼ inch and press.
3. Stitch together with a slipstitch, or machine-stitch all around.

Ohio Star

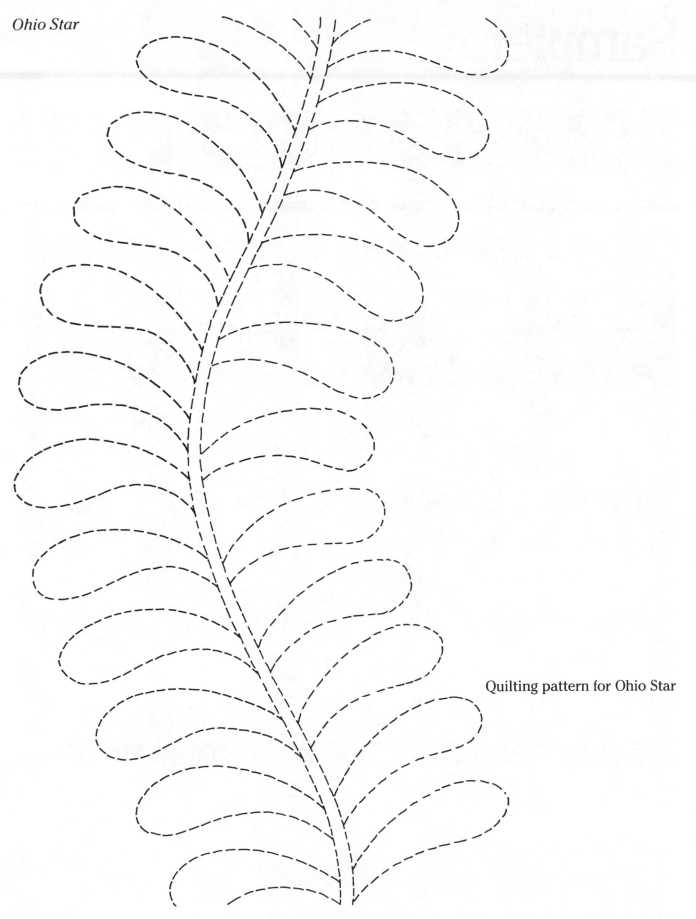

Quilting pattern for Ohio Star

Sampler

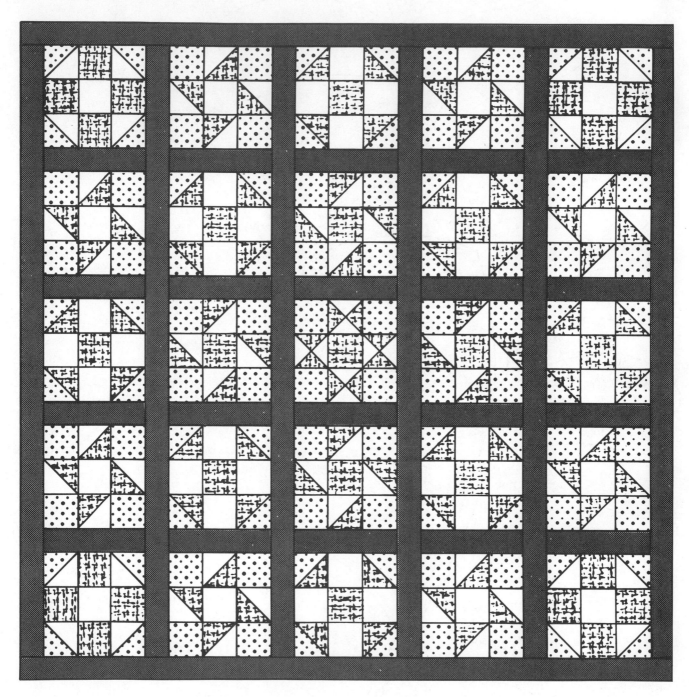

This is an interesting quilt made up of blocks that are made from triangles and squares. Each block is different. Perhaps the most difficult in the book, this quilt will allow you to use all the techniques employed in making the others. Just as with the first quilt, you learn to make one block and then continue in the same way. Once you put one block together you simply do it over and over and then join them. The finished quilt looks harder to make than it actually is. The fall colors and the finished design make it well worth the effort. It measures 57 × 57 inches and is a wonderfully attractive wallhanging.

Materials

(all fabric is 45 inches wide)
1 yard green calico A
1 yard rust calico B
1 yard yello calico C
2 yards brown calico D
3½ yards backing fabric
batting
thread to match fabric colors
needle for hand-quilting

Directions

Begin by cutting all fabric as follows:
A—29 squares 3½ × 3½ inches
A—2 squares 4 × 4 inches
   Cut each of the 2 squares into 4 triangles for a total of 8 triangles.
B—52 squares 3½ × 3½ inches
C—44 squares 3½ × 3½ inches
C—2 squares 4 × 4 inches
   Cut each of the 2 squares into 4 triangles for a total of 8 triangles.
D—2 pieces 2½ × 57½ inches for side borders
D—6 pieces 2½ × 53½ inches for top and bottom borders and lattice strips
D—20 pieces 2½ × 9½ inches for lattice strips

Quick-and-easy triangle method

1. Using C fabric, measure and mark with a pencil 24 squares 4 × 4 inches on the wrong side of the fabric.
2. Draw a diagonal line from one corner to the other through each square as shown in Fig. 1.
3. With right sides facing and raw edges aligned, pin the penciled fabric to a piece of A fabric cut to the same size.
4. Stitch ¼ inch on each side of the diagonal lines as shown in Fig. 1.
5. Cut on all solid lines. You will have 48 squares made up of A and C triangles.
6. Using C fabric, measure and mark 8 squares 4 × 4 inches on the wrong side of the fabric.
7. Draw diagonal lines through the squares from one corner to the other as before.
8. With right sides facing and raw edges aligned, pin the penciled fabric to a piece of B fabric cut to the same size.
9. Stitch ¼ inch on each side of the diagonal lines. Cut on all solid lines. There will be 16 squares made up of B and C fabric.
10. Using A fabric, measure and mark 16 squares 4 × 4 inches on the wrong side of the fabric.
11. Draw a diagonal line through the squares from one corner to the other.
12. With right sides facing and raw edges aligned, pin the penciled fabric to a piece of B fabric cut to the same size.
13. Stitch ¼ inch on each side of the diagonal lines. Cut on all solid lines. There should be 32 squares made from AB triangles.
14. Open seams and press.

Fig. 1

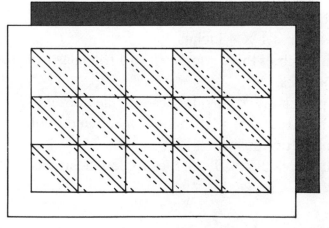

Fig. 2

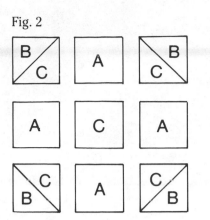

To make block #1

1. With right sides facing and raw edges aligned, stitch a BC square to an A square along one edge as shown in Fig. 2.
2. Open seams and press.
3. Next, join a CB square to the opposite edge of the A square. Open seams and press.
4. With right sides facing and raw edges aligned, stitch an A square to a C square to another A square in the same way. Open all seams and press.
5. With right sides facing and raw edges aligned, stitch a BC square to an A square to a CB square as shown in Fig. 2. Open seams and press.
6. With right sides facing and raw edges aligned, join the first and second row of 3 squares along one long edge. Open seams and press.
7. Join the third row to the second in the same way. Open seams and press.
8. You have just completed block #1 as shown in Fig. 3. Make 4 of these blocks.

Fig. 3

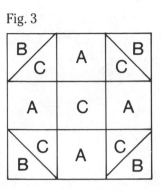

Block 1

To make block #2

1. With right sides facing and raw edges aligned stitch a B square to a CA square along the side edge (see Fig. 4 for arrangement of squares in the block).
2. Open seams and press.
3. Next, join a B square to the CA square to complete the row. Open seams and press.
4. With right sides facing and raw edges aligned, stitch a CA square to a C square to an AC square in the same way. Open all seams and press.
5. With right sides facing and raw edges aligned, stitch a B square to an AC square, followed by another B square. Open seams and press.
6. With right sides facing and raw edges aligned, stitch 3 rows of 3 squares each together along the long edges as shown in Fig. 5. Open seams and press.
7. You have just completed block #2. Make 8 of these blocks.

Fig. 4

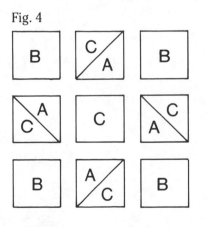

Fig. 5

Block 2

To make block #3

1. With right sides facing and raw edges aligned, stitch a BA square to a C square, followed by an AB square as before. Open seams and press.
2. Continue to join squares as shown in Fig. 6 until you have a block of 9 squares.
3. Open all seams and press.
4. Fig. 7 shows block #3 complete. Make 8 of these blocks.

Fig. 6

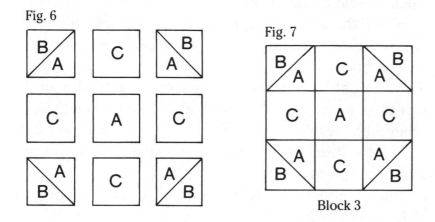

Fig. 7

Block 3

To make block #4

1. Refer to Fig. 8 for the arrangement of squares needed to complete block #4 and stitch each square together as you did for the first 3 blocks.
2. Open all seams and press.
3. Join all 3 rows of 3 blocks each as shown in Fig. 9. Make 4 of these blocks.

Fig. 8

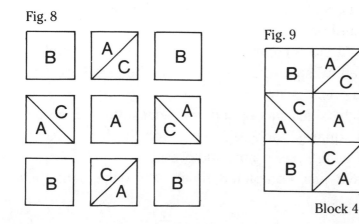

Fig. 9

Block 4

To make block #5

1. With right sides facing and raw edges aligned, stitch a small C triangle to a small A triangle to make triangle AC.

2. Open seams and press.

3. Continue to join triangles to make 8 larger triangles in this way.

4. With right sides facing and raw edges aligned, stitch 2 AC triangles together to form a square as shown in Fig. 10.

5. Open seams and press.

6. Make 3 more squares of 4 triangles each in this way.

7. With right sides facing and raw edges aligned, stitch a B square to a pieced square, followed by another B square as shown in Fig. 10.

8. Open seams and press.

9. Continue to join squares as shown to make up the 3 rows of 3 squares each.

10. With right sides facing and raw edges aligned, stitch rows together along the long edges. Open seams and press.

11. You have just completed block #5 as shown in Fig. 11.

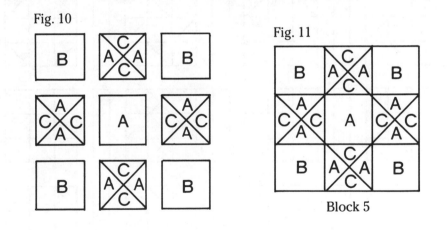

Fig. 10

Fig. 11

Block 5

To make rows

Note: Block #5 is placed in the center of the quilt, which is in the center of the third row as shown in Fig. 12.

1. With right sides facing and raw edges aligned, stitch a block #1 to a D lattice strip (2½ × 9½ inches) along one edge.

2. Open seams and press.

3. Continue to join blocks separated by lattice strips in the order shown in Fig. 12.

4. Open all seams and press. There will be 5 blocks divided by 4 lattice strips in the row.

5. Continue to make 4 more rows following the diagram.

Fig. 12

Row 1

Row 2

Row 3

Row 4

Row 5

154

Joining rows

Note: You will be using the D strips for lattices and borders.

1. With right sides facing and raw edges aligned, stitch row #1 to a D lattice strip (2½ × 53½ inches) as shown in Fig. 13).

2. Open seams and press.

3. With right sides facing and raw edges aligned, stitch row #2 to the long edge of the lattice strip that divides row #1 and row #2. Open seams and press.

4. Continue to join rows separated by lattice strips in this way. Open all seams and press.

Fig. 13

Joining borders

Note: The top and bottom border strips are the remaining $2\frac{1}{2} \times 53\frac{1}{2}$-inch D lattice strips.

1. With right sides facing and raw edges aligned, stitch the top and bottom border pieces D to the top and bottom edge of the quilt top.

2. Open all seams and press.

3. Attach side border D strips ($2\frac{1}{2} \times 57\frac{1}{2}$ inches) to the sides of the quilt top. Open seams and press (see Fig. 13).

Fig. 14

Preparing the backing

1. Cut the batting ½ inch smaller than the quilt top all around.
2. Cut the backing fabric in half so you have two pieces 1¾ yards each.
3. With right sides facing and raw edges aligned, stitch these pieces together along one long edge to create the backing for the quilt.
4. Trim to size, if necessary.
5. Baste the top, batting, and backing together with long stitches through all three layers. Begin at the center of the quilt and baste to each outer corner.
6. Pin or baste around the edges.

Quilting

1. To hand-quilt, begin at the center of the top and work outward, taking small running stitches ¼ inch on both sides of all seam lines of each piece of fabric.
2. Stitch around the seam line of each border strip.
3. To quilt by machine, stitch along the seam line of each piece and the joining seams of each lattice and border strip.

To finish

1. When all quilting is complete, clip the basting stitches away.
2. Fold the raw edges of the top under ¼ inch and press. Turn backing edges to the inside ¼ inch and press.
3. Stitch together with a slipstitch, or machine-stitch all around.

Sources for Quiltmaking Supplies

Since quilting has become so popular across the country, fabric shops are responding with a variety of materials and tools for this purpose. Some well-stocked arts and crafts stores also carry the necessary items.

However, if you can't find what you need there are many mail-order services that have a wide range of items to choose from. Their catalogs are great fun to look through and you'll have the opportunity to discover new and innovative tools for achieving the shortcuts I've used and recommended.

I have contacted the mail-order businesses that are recommended below, and they are most helpful and reliable. If you find it difficult to locate something, one of these sources will gladly help you, or write to me and I'll try to track it down.

Leslie Linsley
Nantucket, MA 02554

Extra Special Products
P.O. Box 777
Greenville, OH 45331

I like the products from this company. Among their extra-special items you'll find a plastic triangle to make perfect 8-point stars and 16-piece Dresden Plates (a popular quilt pattern). They also offer a Lucite ruler pre-marked for mitering perfect corners on your borders. Other specialties are plastic templates, grids, and individual appliqué kits with pre-cut templates. This is an excellent way to learn how to quilt.

Needleart Quilt
2729 Oakwood, N.E.
Grand Rapids, MI 49505

This family-run business has been operating since 1932 and supplies a catalog chock full of all kinds of hard-to-find items. In the supply section I mentioned a quilting thimble to keep fingers intact. This is the company that can send it to you. They also have ¼-inch craft tape for marking seams and water-erasable marking pens. Aside from a good selection of quilting patterns, they sell backing batiste at a reasonable price.

Fairfield Processing Corporation
P.O. Box 1157
Danbury, CT 06810

If you do any crafting you've probably used the batting from Fairfield Processing. Poly-Fil® is the brand name for their quality polyester fiber, which comes in a variety of thicknesses. The quilt batting is packaged in different sizes common to most beds and cribs, but you can also buy it by the yard. All the information is on the package, and it is carried wherever fabric and quilt supplies are sold.

Putnam Company
P.O. Box 310
Walworth, WI 53184

Putnam is another name you often see on batting packages. Their specialty is extra-thick batting for an extra-fluffy quilt. It comes in pre-cut bed sizes or by the yard.

Quilt Patch
261 Main Street
Northboro, MA 01532

If you can't find a good variety of 100% cotton, this is the source for all your calicos, solids, ginghams, and polished cottons. They also carry muslin and cotton sheeting at reasonable prices. If you send $3.00 to the above address, you will receive 400 swatches of fabric and a price list.

One last product you should be aware of is a rotary cutter, which looks like a small pizza-cutting tool. One of the quilt-makers for this book found it invaluable for cutting double layers of fabric strips.